CONTENTS

Chapter 1

INTRODUCTION

Today's Students—Why Aren't They What They Used to Be?

I am a teacher—by training, by experience, and by desire. Teaching is a part of my identity. It is both a profession and a way to serve the Lord, and I wholeheartedly embrace it as such.

The best part about teaching (as most teachers will probably agree) is the interaction I have with my students. That interaction is especially rewarding with students who come into the classroom (or any learning situation) with curiosity, eagerness to test their own abilities, and an open-minded honest attitude about themselves, their relationships with others, and the world at large.

Such students are increasingly rare. The beginning level students—toddlers and lower elementary children—still have a wonderful freshness and eagerness about them. But where I see a rapidly growing number of jaded, worn-out, unenthusiastic, cynical, manipulative, and highly self-critical students is at the upper level of the educational ladder: college. Most of my teaching experience has been with college students and young adults, and it is in that student population that I have seen a dramatic shift over the past two decades.

But isn't *jaded, cynical,* and *self-critical* the perennial definition of college students?

No. Certainly some students in any given class bear those hallmarks to a greater or lesser degree. My concern here is not with the occasional student who comes to college weary with life. Rather, I am speaking of a broad trend I have seen growing in magnitude over the past twenty years. The college students and young adults of today are quite different from the college students of the seventies. Their expectations about life are different. And as a part of that mind-set, their expectations about learning and a college education are different.

Has the educational system changed?

Not a lot. Objectively speaking, I see remarkably little change over the past twenty years—indeed, the last one hundred years—in the processes, structures, and curricula offered in today's elementary, secondary, and college institutions. Although numerous attempts have been made to incorporate various courses and technologies into the mainstream of academe, the general content and methods of "school" have been altered only slightly in this past century.

What has changed, then? The greatest shift has been in the culture as a whole, and in particular, the culture of the American home. By *culture of the home,* I refer to the way in which the family is structured, the customs and routines that form daily life in the home, the flow of power within the home, the amount of communication that occurs among family members, the values and behaviors that are modeled and taught, and the forms of punishment and reward that are meted out.

Teaching hasn't changed nearly as much as parenting has.

A Dramatic Shift in Student Profiles

Two decades ago, relatively few of my students came from

- families marked by divorce and remarriage,

- single-parent families, or
- families in which both parents worked outside the home.

Although abuse may have occurred in the homes from which my students came twenty years ago, that abuse tended not to be discussed, was rarely used as an excuse, and nearly always was viewed as something unfortunate to be overcome. Few of my students in the 1970s saw themselves as victims of their pasts, but rather, if abuse had occurred, they regarded themselves as survivors. For the most part, they spoke highly of their parents and childhoods and were eager to embrace their own bright futures. Some were not in favor of their parents' lifestyles or the culture as a whole, but even these students tended to hold the position that their parents had done the best they could, and that they would do even better as parents one day.

Virtually none of my students twenty years ago came to college with experience in habitual drug use, extensive premarital sexual experience, or association with friends who were addicted to drugs or alcohol. Twenty years ago, most of my students had spent at least as many of their nonschool hours playing and reading as they had in "watching life." Very few of them had seen more than one or two R-rated or X-rated movies, much less the thousands of murders, rapes, and other violent actions that today's students have seen routinely on television by the time they leave high school. The music to which they listened, for the most part, tended to be rooted in themes of love and social change, rather than themes of social upheaval and personal violence or oppression.

Perhaps more important, most of my students came to college expecting to gain, to grow, to excel, and to leave college with the skills and knowledge that would enable them to succeed in a life of their own choosing.

And today?

The majority of my students now come from broken, single-parent, or two-parent-at-work families. They have drastically more "street experience" than many of their college professors—that is, experience with sex, drugs, and violence. They have moved more often and have lived in multiple family structures. They are excellent observers of life and work but somewhat reluctant participants. They have seen hundreds of movies, watched countless television programs, and listened to thousands of songs riddled with behaviors that, on the whole, our culture still condemns as aberrant, obscene, distasteful, immoral, or illegal. Sadly, many see college as a must-endure torture chamber that is intended to launch them into a rather bleak job market, where they will work at less-than-desired wages for an uncertain length of time. Others have very unrealistic expectations that they will have it all and be it all with very little effort on their part. Most believe society owes them something, although their opinions about just what is owed tend to vary widely.

A very high percentage of my students today do not believe they have control over their own destinies, but rather, that they have control only over their immediate environments, friends, and free-time schedules. They can control their parties but not their lives. Others tend to see their destinies as a product of luck, and those who hold this position often see themselves as destined for a charmed life.

Before you conclude that I am writing off the present generation of students, let me assure you that I still do have a good number of students who embody the old traits of moral goodness, high hopes, and positive, healthy self-esteem. It is the fact that these students still exist that motivated me to write this book.

What is it that makes some of my students optimistic, psychologically healthy, and eager learners while others seem so rooted in pessimism, dysfunction, and despair?

In search of answers, I have conversed with literally hundreds of college students during the past few years, asking them to tell me about their families, their early years, and their self-perceptions. And I simply listened. I wanted to hear their stories, as completely as they were willing to tell them to me. Many of them shared willingly with tears, some shared reluctantly until trust had been established between us, some shared a gusher of pent-up anger or hatred. Others seemed depressed and defeated. A few seemed genuinely eager to embrace their futures.

Some shared only bits and pieces of their lives over several years while others shared more in long, flowing, after-midnight conversations. Most of them shared their life stories with me outside the formal classroom—over coffee at a diner, in my living room, on walks, or during overnight school-related retreats and field trips.

From these many conversations I drew two conclusions:

What a parent teaches a child has far more influence on a child's future than anything a classroom teacher teaches.
And . . .
Parents bear the primary responsibility for teaching their children the most important things their children need to know.

To some, these may seem like statements of the obvious. But surprisingly, many parents believe that the school bears the *primary* responsibility for teaching their children. A good percentage of parents fully expect the school to do it all—not only teach reading, writing, and arithmetic (and, in today's world, computer-related skills), but also teach culture, self-esteem, manners, appropriate sexual behavior, drug awareness, job skills, values, safety, personal hygiene, patriotism, and much more. These parents expect the school to teach a child both how to think and what to think, rather than only presenting information about which to think.

In terms of time and training, it seems to make sense for parents to yield power to the school system and expect more from their children's teachers. After all, a child today spends far more of his waking hours with a teacher or after-school caretaker than with his own parents—as much as two times more between the ages of five and fifteen on any given school day. After all, teachers are trained how to teach; parents rarely are trained how to parent. After all, teachers are the role models of today's society and, as such, have great influence over a child's life.

All of these statements are true . . . but only to a degree.

At the very outset of this discussion, let's take a realistic look at what teachers can and cannot do.

What Teachers Can and Cannot Do

A teacher *can* present facts, concepts, principles, rules or laws, and procedures to students. Name virtually any discipline, and the standard curriculum comes down to a presentation of these very basic elements. A teacher can build a good case in attempting to convince a student to accept certain facts, concepts, principles, rules, and procedures as being valid and reliable. The methods are those of presentation, conversation, experimentation, application, examination, evaluation, and remediation. Teachers are bound by time and space, however, to how and what they can present of a body of knowledge that is growing exponentially every day.

Stated another way, teachers present information and test for a student's comprehension or memorization of *a selected set of information.* This is an important point to consider. Even the best schoolteachers, equipped with the most thorough curriculum and using the most innovative methods, cannot teach a child all the facts, concepts, principles, rules, and procedures necessary to cope with life. The knowledge explosion of the last two centuries has resulted in only a *very small fraction* of the world's knowledge being presented in even the best K-12 curriculum.

Teachers have attempted to compensate for this by teaching students how to learn: how to study, how to conduct research, and how to adapt to changing ideas and technologies. More and more emphasis is being placed on learning skills rather than on content. Yet a teacher has no time-tested, reliable way of creating or testing for genuine *understanding*— which includes a full incorporation of information into a student's thinking, feeling, and behavioral patterns. A teacher has little opportunity to see how a student lives out the information acquired in the classroom, either through immediate application or in the years to come. At best, teachers *hope* they are teaching students how to learn and how to adapt to a changing world. Whether they are succeeding is something that won't be known for perhaps decades.

A teacher can insist that a child or youth adult sit up, stay awake, be quiet, respond orally or in writing, and take a test. A teacher cannot insist that a child *learn or remember.*

A teacher can present a wide variety of values to students, including the opportunity to engage in value-oriented simulation exercises. Teachers, however, do *not* have the privilege of declaring to students what they personally hold to be true. Indeed, no one teacher has a handle on full and absolute truth. Each teacher has a personal and highly individualized perspective on or relationship with truth.

In reality, teachers do *not* spend more time with a child than his parents do over the course of a decade, in spite of what many think. Children are only in school about half the days of any given year. Any one teacher impacts a student's life only for a few hours a week, a few weeks of their lives. Rarely does a teacher have a mentoring relationship with a student that lasts longer than a year (the exception being, perhaps, teachers who specialize in music, art, dance, and so forth).

Furthermore, teachers and students relate in a limited environment. A student rarely sees her teacher "out of uniform" or during off hours. A student, for the most part, has little understanding of a teacher's full life—personal relationships, hobbies, home, family members, church, memberships in other organizations, or what her early years were like. The same goes for a teacher's view of a student. Although a teacher may confer with parents periodically, a teacher rarely has full knowledge of a student's home, church, or neighborhood life. The normal parent-teacher relationship is one that is nearly always limited to the hours, physical space, information, and tasks of the classroom or laboratory, with an occasional field trip thrown in for good measure.

Furthermore, a teacher with thirty students does not spend hours of quality time with each student each week. Oh, how most teachers wish that were possible! Most teachers teach the whole of a class or class subgroup and then spend time with problem students who need extra help. The average student receives less than five minutes of one-to-one teacher attention in any given week. Good and exceptional students tend to receive less personalized teacher time than poor or problematic students.

In sum, then, any one teacher sees any one student only

part of the time, deals with only part of the student's life, and presents only part of the information a student needs to know in facing *all* of life.

What most teachers give to their students is good instruction . . . but it is very, very, *very* limited in scope—and far more limited than many parents want to acknowledge.

Those parents who see teachers as having the primary responsibility for their child's education are parents who tend to regard formal schooling as the foundation of learning to which they add their own bits of knowledge and experience. The exact opposite is true. The *home* is the ground of learning, to which teachers add a very specialized set of information.

The difference in perspective is a dramatic one. If you have never given thought to how you perceive your child's schooling, I encourage you to do so. Ask yourself:

Do I see the teacher and the school as the primary source of my child's education and myself as only an accessory in the learning process?
Or . . .
Do I see myself as the primary source of my child's education and expect the school to supplement what I teach?

The contention of this book is that parents are the *primary* teachers of a child from birth to maturity (which, mentally, biologically, and culturally tends to be eighteen years of age). The family and home are the primary place of schooling. Furthermore, all that schools and teachers present to a child is ultimately the responsibility of that child's parents.

The School as Enemy, the Teacher as Alien?

A growing number of parents seem to feel that the public school their child attends is more like a foreign land than a reflection of their own home or neighborhood. What they feel is very often rooted in objective reality.

The culture of many homes is no longer reflected in the culture of the public school. Power, communication, status, and rewards often flow in a manner completely opposite to that of the home. The school is not a safe, positive, esteem-building, value-reinforcing extension of the home for many of this nation's children. Unfortunately, in many cases, the home itself no longer provides a safe, positive, esteem-building, value-reinforcing environment.

Public schoolteachers tend to be as dismayed about their schools as concerned parents are. In my experience with elementary and secondary schoolteachers, I have found that public schoolteachers strongly decry the presence of violence and the lack of disciplinary authority in many schools. They, too, feel as if they are the aliens in a foreign land. They are constrained by a system that now insists they fill the roles of police, preacher (of many religions without prejudice), and therapist, in addition to the role of classroom teacher. Many of them simply burn out after years of struggling to cope with a job description that is far beyond the scope of educator.

A growing number of teachers also do not agree with the set of information that the government now insists be taught in the classroom. Given a choice, they would slice the information pie in a much different way.

It is no fluke that private school enrollment has risen dramatically in the last decade, and that some of the finest and most moral teachers are moving out of the public sector and into the private sector, sometimes leaving education for another field altogether. That shift is a clear indication that the discrepancy between the culture of the home and the culture of the society at large is growing, not diminishing.

If your child is in a public school, her classroom teacher probably feels much the same frustration that you do about the system and is far more likely to be an ally than an alien. With only rare exceptions, she wants the very best for your child and is willing to give her best effort to provide a quality presentation of facts, concepts, principles, rules, and procedures. As a parent, however, you need to understand that teachers in the public school system today are required by law and by school board mandate to do far more than teach basic information as innovatively as possible. In many cases, they are required to keep records and to present information for which they have received no training and have no time.

Again, the problem lies in a basic misconception that the school bears the primary and main responsibility for a child's education. The school cannot, does not, and never will have that position, unless cradle-to-grave institutionalization becomes the norm in our society.

Please do not conclude that I am advocating private education or home schooling as the only way to go. I am not. But parents must define the education they desire their children to receive: This is what I want my child to learn and this is how I want my child to be educated. Then, on behalf of their children, they bear the responsibility for securing the best schooling and teachers possible. Parents can no longer expect the culture at large to mirror their own culture. They no longer can expect the public school to reinforce the values, structures, or information that is emphasized in their homes. They must recognize the discrepancies that exist and make schooling choices that best reflect their desires.

If thinking of yourself as your child's primary educator seems overwhelming, then see yourself as your child's *educational manager*. Your role is to manage and supervise thoroughly the education that your child receives—from birth to the day your child is no longer under your authority.

Exercising this management responsibility effectively within the public school system is possible, but agreement from other parents generally is required to achieve major comprehensive results.

In some instances, such involvement may take the form of attendance at school board meetings, participation on textbook review committees, active membership in the Parent Teacher Association (PTA), or volunteering as an aide in your child's classroom. In other instances, involvement might be expressed through voting in school board elections or running for school board positions, by means of official protests, through shared decisionmaking about which teachers your child should have, or by conferring regularly with your child's teacher. Use whatever means are available to you to exercise your right to be your child's *education manager*.

A recent survey of some of the nation's top schools revealed an interesting correlation. The most successful schools in the nation—as determined by student test scores, student morale, and opinions of parents—were the schools that had high parental involvement and support. The role of parents in helping at schools, supporting school activities, and attending school functions far outweighed all other factors, including the soundness of curriculum, the degree of safety and discipline, or the amount of financial resources pumped into the school. Highly successful schools were found in all areas of the nation and in neighborhoods with widely varying socioeconomic levels. Successful schools were clearly those in which the educational process was seamless between home and school. They were schools in which parents took an active rather than passive role.

What About the Christian School?

If your child goes to a Christian or private school, be careful that you aren't lulled into a false sense of security and that you don't pass the buck to the school.

Never assume that solely because your child attends a school founded on beliefs basic to your life that your child's teacher is the *primary* teacher of those beliefs. As in the public schools, your child's teacher is still bound by the constraints of time, space, and curriculum. The teacher still has a limited amount of time to present massive amounts of information. He or she has only limited access to your child and an impact on only a segment of your child's world. There tends to be very little variance between public and private schools in the content presented. Indeed, surveys through the years have revealed that many Christian and private schools use the same textbooks and follow the same curriculum formats as their public school counterparts. The main difference between Christian schools and public schools seems to lie in the value orientation of the teachers and administrators and in the amount of discipline exacted in the school.

It is precisely in Christian and private schools that a good many parents make the assumption that they are doing all they need to do regarding the education of their children. Because the parents are making sacrifices to send the child to the school, and they trust the values and standards of the school, the conclusion is that the school will also be the child's primary place of learning. This simply isn't the case. The child's primary place of learning is still the home and family. The parent is still the child's teacher, first and foremost, and the parent still bears the responsibility first and foremost for presenting information and managing the child's education. No school and no church can take the place of the home and family as a learning environment.

A Word About Child-Care Workers

As never before, parents today are relying upon hired caregivers to help them in their parenting. The caregiver may be a baby-sitter, nanny, governess, day care worker, or relative. Most of these workers are paid for their services and work within a fixed set of guidelines to which a parent tacitly or contractually agrees.

For the most part, hired caregivers specialize in *cage maintenance*—a harsh phrase, perhaps, but an accurate one nevertheless. Hired caregivers nearly always are given boundaries by parents—boundaries of time, space, and relationship—in which to relate to the child. Parents give hired caregivers such instructions as, "Care for my child within the home (or day care center). Do not leave this environment with my child unless you ask my permission. Teach my child what the specified curriculum says and nothing more. Don't punish my child. Feed him regularly. I'll be here at seven each morning and be back by seven o'clock at night." Hence, the term *cage*: a space, a time frame, and a relationship marked by fairly rigid boundaries.

What the caregiver generally does is that which is basic to a child's health, happiness, and survival. Hence, the word *maintenance.* Parents tend to tell a caregiver: You watch, feed, put to bed, play with, teach certain skills to, and change the diapers of my child during these hours, in this place, for this amount of money. Hired caregivers rarely are authorized to do what is necessary to help a child reach his full potential or to excel.

Rarely does a parent expect a hired caregiver to teach a child right from wrong, to give meaningful punishment or reward, to isolate aptitudes or compel curiosity, to do what he or she believes is important in challenging a child to stretch and grow mentally, emotionally, and physically, or to instill values, beliefs, or cultural norms.

Hired caregivers provide parenting at only the most rudimentary level. They often are not true teachers, and they very rarely are true parents.

Don't expect even a live-in, full-time nanny or governess to teach your child the most important lessons of life. He or she does not have the final authority to do that job and rarely is equipped or willing to do it even if given that authority.

You Are Your Child's Number One Teacher

Again, we come back to the same premise: As a parent, you are your child's primary teacher. You have the responsibility for teaching life lessons to your child in a way that no one else can.

The good news is this: *You can do it!* Not only do you have responsibility for filling the role of teacher and educational manager, but you have the built-in opportunity and ability. There are certain lessons that are vital to a child's success in life that you are best equipped to teach as a parent. In fact, you can teach them far better than any schoolteacher or hired caregiver.

This does not mean that you need to have formal training as a teacher. It does mean that you need to be aware of your responsibility to teach and that you desire to do the best possible job of teaching.

Don't be dismayed at the prospect of being a teacher. Chances are, you are already filling the role and doing so fairly well.

We'll explore why and in what ways you are your child's best teacher. But first, let's define the good student.

Chapter 2

The Good Student

Madeline had a smile that could light up an entire room. I first met her while I was a graduate student working on a master's degree at a major university. As many graduate students, I had received financial aid in the form of a teaching assistantship with an obligation to teach two freshman-level sections of a speech class. I loved being a T.A.—it was *teaching*. And Madeline quickly became one of my favorite students.

Madeline was half Vietnamese and half French, named in honor of her paternal grandmother in Paris, a woman who had died shortly before Madeline's birth in Saigon. Her father had died a few years before she came to the United States, not as a result of the war but in a commercial shipping accident.

Much of Madeline's life had been overshadowed by the Vietnam War, of course. She and her family had been forced to move several times to escape its ravages. I found it amazing that she had managed to excel in her schooling despite such family and social turmoil, and that she had the fortitude to move thousands of miles away from her mother and younger sister to pursue a university degree.

Madeline was a bright and eager student. She never missed a class or sloughed off an assignment. She often came to me after class to ask clarifying questions, wanting to make sure that she understood concepts and instructions thoroughly. On a day when I asked my class to prepare a simple show-and-tell speech, she brought a lovely Vietnamese instrument to class and sang her speech. Her approach was innovative and bold; this was a young woman apparently willing to take big risks. Even though she spoke in broken English at first, she readily offered ideas and opinions in class discussions. The other students responded warmly to her and admired her general optimism.

The first assignment I made was this: "Come before the class, pause, look at the class with a smile, and give us the one word that has the greatest meaning for you. Then, pause, smile again at us, and return to your seat." Through the years I have been surprised by how much I learn about my students from the word choices they make. Madeline's word was poignant: *Mother.*

I asked her later to tell me why she had chosen that word. She replied with simple eloquence, "Have greatest longing for Mother, so must have greatest meaning for word." Madeline knew that she would not see her mother again for nearly four years. Her homeland was reeling from an American military withdrawal and the takeover of leadership by forces in Hanoi. Nothing in her life seemed stable or reliable, and yet Madeline felt very positive about her future. She still felt a strong sense of belonging to her family, and she believed implicitly that somehow, in some way, she was going to make a difference in her nation.

She made high grades in my class, and I admired how quickly her English improved to the point that she rarely made a grammatical or vocabulary error. I asked her once how long it took her to complete a particular assignment. She smiled and said, "Until I know." Her roommate later told me that Madeline often stayed up until two or three o'clock in the morning, poring over her textbooks with a dictionary close at hand.

Madeline and I had a number of conversations through

the year, even after she was no longer a student in my class. I came to see that she was not merely a student taking classes. Madeline had a mission: to complete a baccalaureate degree. She was compelled to succeed, not only at school but at life. She owed it to her family and, therefore, to herself. This did not keep her from having a social life, but she maintained a very careful balance between time spent studying and time spent with friends. Madeline had priorities and goals.

Mike, on the other hand, had neither priorities nor goals related to his studies.

His first words to me were, "What can a blonde broad teach me?" I responded candidly, "With that attitude, probably nothing."

I hate to admit that I was probably right. I have no sense whatsoever that Mike learned anything in my class on newswriting.

He went by the name of Michael Louis, even though his legal name was Mike. He thought the more formal first name, coupled with his middle name, made him appear intelligent and literary. Appearance was important to Mike—far more than substance.

Mike came to class fairly regularly, because more than three absences resulted in an automatic lowering of the grade for the course. He missed exactly three classes. He showed up exactly nine minutes late for class. Ten minutes late classified a student as tardy and tardies could accumulate to become an absence. (The absence and time stipulations were not my design but the school's.) He sat at his desk in my classroom, but he slept, read a novel, or worked on an unrelated class project. In other words, Mike barely scraped by—keeping rules to the letter of the law but hardly in spirit.

He earned a C in the course and argued for every point related to that grade. He rarely turned in his assignments on time, and few of his assignments were complete. As part of the course, I conducted a half-hour, one-to-one tutorial with each student to go over in detail a writing sample of their choice. Halfway through my session with Mike, he got up as if to walk out and announced bluntly that I was wrong in my grading and didn't know anything about editing, much less literary style.

I responded, "Mike, uncapped letters at the beginning of sentences, split infinitives, and subject-verb disagreements have nothing to do with style. But I'm willing to hear you out about this matter of style. Talk to me about the style you want to achieve and your goals as a writer. Talk to me about what it is that you really want out of this course and out of college."

He sat down and, much to my surprise, unloaded. Michael Louis didn't remotely want to be in college. He longed to strap on a backpack and hit the trails of Wyoming, fishing for his dinner from stream to stream and writing the next great American novel along the way. The last thing he wanted was a nine-to-five job, a house and mortgage in the suburbs, a wife and family, and a van to park in a two-car garage.

"Then why are you in college?" I asked. "Why are you taking a journalism course?"

His reply was eloquent, the one word that held for him the greatest meaning and for which he had the greatest loathing: *Mom.*

"Mom?" I asked with a surprised laugh. "I'm sorry I laughed, but that's the last reason I expected to hear. I probably would have been less surprised if you had said, 'Dad.' "

Mike grimaced. "Yeah, it probably *is* Dad . . . ultimately."

Mike's dad had skipped out a few years earlier without any explanation or any subsequent communication. Mom had held her son hostage in the intervening years, expecting him to be her emotional support and eventually her financial provider. Mike was in college because Mom was looking for a future meal ticket.

Mike saw no future for himself, only dreams that would never be lived out. He resented hearing anything from anyone. Any correction, including proofreading marks on ten paragraphs of news copy, was simply one more extension of Mom telling him what to do. He was a hostile, bitter young man.

At first, other students found Mike's sarcasm clever and witty, but I noticed that none of them ever walked into or out of the classroom with Mike. As the semester wore on, they simply ignored him. Mike had no give-and-take with his peers, just as he had no give-and-take with his professors. He had only pat answers and seething anger.

What Type of Student Is Your Child?

Madeline and Mike stand at opposite poles of a "good student—bad student" continuum.

In educational circles, much is made of "objectives." Nearly all teachers are required at some point to write out behavioral objectives related to their course materials or lesson plans. These are statements about what the teacher expects a student to be able to do after receiving instruction. Properly stated behavioral objectives must include measurable and observable behavior.

As we discuss the role of parents as teachers, it is important to state what type of "student" we are hoping to produce. Ask yourself:

- What is it that I want my child to *do* as a student?
- What behaviors related to learning do I want my child to exhibit on a day-to-day and a lifelong basis?
- What intellectual qualities do I want my child to develop?

Unfortunately, very few parents ask any of those questions. Instead, they make general statements about their child's educational goals:

- I want my child to do his best.
- I want my child to learn what is important for him to know so he can get a good job.
- I want my child to study whatever makes her happy.
- I want my child to have at least a B average so he can get into a good college.

These are not true *behavioral* objectives related to learning. They describe outcomes but not attributes related directly to the process of learning.

How do you know if your child is doing his best? How do you and your child know what is important for her to learn at age eight so she can get a good job at age twenty-three? How do you know if your child is intellectually happy? What kinds of courses are important, and what does a B average mean in terms of your child's abilities and level of effort?

Describing the Good Student

The good student has the following ten characteristics.

1. The good student sees himself as part of a larger whole.

He therefore shows respect to other people and accommodates both their presence and their ideas and expressions of feeling.

In the classroom, a good student shows respect for teachers and fellow classmates, does not interrupt them when they are talking, listens to their ideas, allows them to express themselves fully before responding, and enjoys the group process of learning. A good student is one who willingly participates in group learning activities.

By contrast, the bad student is one who has no use for anybody's opinion but her own and refuses to acknowledge the validity of others' expressing themselves fully.

This is not to say that a student must agree with every position put forth, but she does need to recognize that as part of the academic and general democratic processes each person has the right to express her opinions.

2. The good student regards all people and all situations as potentially beneficial and engages readily in conversation in search of the good that might be gained from each interchange. He is willing to learn from others vicariously.

In the classroom, such a student enjoys dialogue and debate but openly acknowledges his own weak arguments or unsubstantiated evidence. A good student is one who speaks his own mind. The good student does not necessarily believe he needs to learn everything or test every hypothesis through personal experience but, rather, acknowledges that the experiences of others can be applied to his life.

The bad student, by comparison, goes into new situations *not* expecting to learn anything applicable to her life. She has a closed mind and sees new ideas as threatening. She believes that only what she personally has experienced is valid.

3. The good student is curious about life and, in expressing that curiosity, eagerly asks questions, conducts thorough research, tests hypotheses, enjoys the process of discovery, and pushes toward the boundaries of his own potential.

In the classroom, the good student asks for clarification and expansion of information, researches answers to problems and questions with an intent toward gaining knowledge more than completing an assignment. The good student is one who wants to see how much she can do, learn, and grow, without regard to a specific grade or test score. The good student is one who enjoys the process of learning, not simply the completion of a course. The good student knows how and from whom to ask questions that give him the answers he needs.

The bad student is more concerned with the "pass" level than with his own potential. He rarely asks questions, other than "do we have to know this for the test?"

4. The good student pursues what is healthful and what is helpful, both to herself and to others and, toward that end, has a criterion for determining standards of wholeness and goodness, an ability to see information as incremental and sequential, and an ability to apply information to life.

The good student develops an ability to judge between important and unimportant data, to discern right from wrong, and prioritize time, activities, and the expenditure of energy toward reaching goals. The good student is capable of making outlines, discerns which information is most worthy of being committed to memory, sees how to apply information to life, and has an ability to see how one set of information builds upon or is necessary to other information. The good student is generous in sharing what she knows to be healthful and helpful to others and expresses that generosity by readily offering her opinions and ideas but not in an abusive, dishonest, or manipulative manner. The good student neither plagiarizes nor cheats.

The bad student is concerned only with the completion of an assignment and sees little or no application of information to his life. He has little ability to prioritize information, make outlines or time schedules, or break assignments down into component segments. As a result, he often finds himself in a time bind before test dates or due dates for major assignments. He seeks assistance completing assignments without regard to whether his actions are intellectually or morally honest.

5. *The good student accepts responsibility for the grades he earns and sees them in relationship to achievement.*

The good student admits, "I earned this grade," rather than complains, "The teacher gave me this grade." The good student sees a correlation between achievement and these three factors: effort, study and learning skills, and innate abilities.

The bad student blames teachers for her poor classroom performance.

6. *The good student pursues excellence and seeks to achieve it in his own life.*

The good student seeks the greatest amount of knowledge possible. The bad student does only the bare minimum required.

7. *The good student can form rational arguments and can both create and understand a line of reasoning and logic. As part of that ability, she has a good vocabulary and solid language skills.*

The good student is capable of using evidence to make decisions. The good student is one who has well-developed reading, writing, speaking, and listening skills. The bad student relies primarily on intuition or emotions.

8. *The good student recognizes that perfection is not possible, either in herself or others, and, at the same time, is aware of her own special talents and abilities.*

The good student does not expect to excel in each pursuit but rather gives his best effort to determine his own areas of high achievement. The good student does not compete with others as much as he competes with himself. The good student regards the future as being bright, but with realistic expectations. The poor student prefers bell-curve grading because it gives her the optimum chance of earning a C. She rarely sees her own unique gifts and aptitudes and frequently suffers from low self-esteem.

9. The good student refuses to take the label of **victim** *or to follow undeserving leaders.*

The good student stands up for his own opinions and ideas, and refuses to be bullied. The bad student, by contrast, withdraws into silence and is easily swayed by strongly voiced opinions and often becomes an ideological "follower."

10. The good student seeks the highest possible truth and chooses to speak truthfully.

The good student is honest with himself about what he knows and doesn't know and admits when he doesn't know something. The good student is always in pursuit of more information.

The bad student is content with the knowledge he has and tends to think that it is not only sufficient for himself but also for all others. The bad student rarely pursues any course of study not prescribed as essential by a person in power.

In brief, the hallmark characteristics of good and bad students are:

The Good Student

Diligent	Optimistic
Open-minded	Ambitious (in pursuing excellence)
Realistic	Thoughtful (rational, with good language skills)
Curious and creative	Independent thinking
Discerning	Intellectually honest
Problem-solving	Decisive
Responsible	Realistic but hopeful

The Bad Student

Closed-minded Disengaged	Defensive (blames others)
Pessimistic	Satisfied with minimum standards
Incapable of sustained effort	Emotional (with minimal language skills)
Dependent on others for innovation or leadership	Satisfied with minimal intellectual effort Unrealistically hopeless about the future

These traits manifest themselves in various related behaviors. They are not automatic predictors of generalized school achievement. A good student can flunk a particular quiz or test. Or she can limit her focus to only one subject and become very narrow in her achievement. For the most part, however, a good student is going to make good grades and pursue a college degree (and perhaps a specialized graduate degree) and maintain a lifelong desire to learn, which will help her greatly in achieving personal fulfillment and job satisfaction. In the same manner, the bad student is likely to settle for poor grades, be satisfied with minimal levels of schooling, and think it unnecessary to pursue any education after that minimal level has been achieved.

More important, these characteristics are *inner qualities,* not outer behaviors that result from the schooling process. Good students achieve more in good schools, but good schools do not necessarily produce only good students.

This idea is critical for parents: *You do not send your child to school as a blank slate on which the teacher writes the traits of a good student.* A teacher might help a student become a better decision maker or problem solver, but almost always the student already comes to school with a desire to make decisions and solve problems. A teacher might enhance a child's creativity and introduce new means of expression, but in all likelihood the child already has a creative bent. A teacher might help a child become more responsible doing his homework, but for the most part the student already has a good work ethic.

What Children Do Bring to School as Students

Teachers work with both good and bad students, but they do not create either variety.

I once had a parent tell me that her son had been an excellent student until he entered the fourth grade. "His fourth grade teacher ruined Ricky," she said.

"How did she do that?" I asked.

"She was a very strict disciplinarian, and she destroyed his interest in school," she replied. "He started daydreaming, and he never did click back into what was happening in the classroom."

Personally, I love daydreamers. I did a lot of daydreaming in school as a child. Daydreaming students are often among the brightest and most creative students in a class. I wanted to explore that line of thought further.

"What did Ricky daydream about?" I asked.

"Oh, I never asked him," she said. "In fact, I never saw him daydreaming. The teacher said he was a daydreamer who didn't pay attention. She punished him for that by making him sit in the front of the room so that all he could see was the blackboard."

"Do you have any idea why she did that?" I asked.

"I suppose so he'd have fewer distractions and could concentrate better. The fact was, however, that he was bored out of his mind, and he resented sitting in front of the class. All he did was daydream more."

"Sounds like a vicious cycle," I commented.

"Exactly," she said. "The more he daydreamed, the worse he did, and the more he got into trouble. The more he got into trouble, the more he withdrew."

"And what did you do?" I asked.

"What could I do?" she replied, miffed that I would ask such a question. "She was the teacher."

There was so much this mother could have done. But I also suspected there was more to the story than she had told me. Several months later in a very different setting, I asked her to tell me more of her life story. I learned that she and her husband had divorced when Ricky was quite young—to be precise, in the summer before he entered fourth grade.

Ricky probably hadn't been daydreaming. Most likely he had been worrying! He hadn't learned to let his mind wander from a schooling process or teacher discipline. He had learned it from the upheaval at home. Had this mother talked to the teacher about Ricky's situation, the teacher might have recognized Ricky's need to engage in activities that would keep his mind *fully* occupied.

One teacher with a similar problem allowed the child to sit in the back of the room and write, draw, or read independently. Those exercises allowed the child to express feelings in a positive, overt way while keeping the child's mind fully absorbed in school-related activities.

Had Ricky's mother been more sensitive to what was happening in her son, and had she felt a sense of responsibility for Ricky's profile as a good student, she might have suggested to the teacher that Ricky be allowed to read challenging materials or work puzzles at his desk.

Ricky's teacher didn't cause him to become disengaged from the classroom. He brought the propensity from home.

What Does Not Limit the Good Student

There are prerequisites for a child to become a good student—but not the ones you might think.

1. The traits of a good student are not limited to an academic field.

The good chemistry student bears the same hallmarks as the good student in music, literature, nursing, horticulture, or tennis.

2. These traits are not linked to a person's innate intellectual ability or IQ.

I have known extremely brilliant young people with IQ scores off the top of the chart who were poor students. At the same time, I have had students who were average in their innate intellectual talent but who were very good students.

They truly maximized their abilities and became very successful both in school and in life.

3. These traits are not linked to any one level of schooling.

A good student in elementary school tends to be a good student in high school and then a good student in college and, ultimately, a good student throughout life. These traits are not bound to any one age level or grade.

4. The traits are not linked to socioeconomic levels.

I have had both good and bad students from wealthy, influential homes and I've had both from low-income homes.

5. These traits are not limited to any one type of schooling or method of instruction.

Good students tend to perform equally well in open, self-directed, free-form instructional settings as well as traditional, highly focused, teacher-led, task-specific settings.

6. The traits of a good student are not related to morality.

I am in no way drawing a correlation between a good student and a good person.

The good student is a person who gets the most out of an instructional setting, including the most joy and personal satisfaction. A good student may transfer these benefits to other areas of life—career and hobbies—but he or she does not necessarily pursue righteousness or seek a relationship with God. An open, curious, ambitious student can pursue a life of crime just as easily as a life of virtue. The intellectually lazy, dependent, uncreative person is capable of faith and a moral lifestyle and may know the joy of personal salvation.

One of the best students I ever had turned out to be one of the most morally corrupt. Pam was a business student who gravitated toward journalism because she saw big money in the field of advertising. She was an eager learner and a quick study. Within a matter of two semesters, she had mastered the essentials of marketing research, good graphic design, and advertising copywriting. She had excellent problem-solving and decisionmaking skills and was extremely ambitious. Once out of school she rapidly moved into control of both the advertising manager and business manager positions at a local advertising agency. Four years later she was arrested for embezzlement and intent to fraud the Internal Revenue Service.

Being a good student and being a good citizen are both matters of choice, and parents influence that decision.

7. The traits of a good student have nothing to do with race or ethnicity.

A myth seems to have arisen in recent years that students of some cultures automatically are better than those of others and, in particular, that Oriental students are intellectually superior to student of other races. That is not borne out by intelligence test scores, although it has been concluded from some achievement tests. Upon close examination, a cultural difference in performance is nearly always the result of *effort*, not intellect. Oriental parents do exhibit a greater tendency to insist that their children make schooling a top priority and that they give greater time and effort to their studies. Elementary-level students in Japan, as an example, spend twenty-five percent more hours in school each year than do elementary-level students in the United States.

8. The traits of a good student have no relation to religious preference.

When it comes to having an open mind, being curious

and creative, being ambitious and thoughtful, thinking independently, discerning nuances of meaning, and being realistic but hopeful about the future, I have found virtually no generalized differences along religious lines.

Highly religious students do not tend to be good students to any greater extent than students from agnostic or casually religious backgrounds. Atheists are not better students than fundamentalists.

9. The traits of a good student have no relation to gender.

Equal numbers of girls and boys are either good or bad students.

In summation, traits of a good or bad learner—readily observed by classroom and other behaviors—are resident within a person without regard to age, income, race, culture, sex, religion, grade in school, or field of study.

There is a correlation, however, between these traits and the home.

The Link Is to the Home

Parents send their children off to school with a mind-set for being a good or bad student, whether they intend to or not.

Growing up in a small town, I had two very close friends who lived near my house: Joannie and Anne. We were all within six weeks of being the same age.

Joannie was a cousin. Of the three of us, she was the most timid or, in retrospect, perhaps the most obedient. Anne and I were forever talking her into climbing the tree, riding her bicycle beyond the boundary set by my mother, or allowing herself to be pulled along on her skates behind one of our bikes. Anne and I *pushed* Joannie into doing things she otherwise would not have done.

Her parents never did. They *encouraged* Joannie, applauded and praised her. They believed she could learn, and they expected her to be a good student, whether in vacation Bible school, regular school, or at the local swimming pool. They didn't expect her to excel, but, rather, they encouraged her to learn all there was to learn. Perhaps because Joannie was a bit shy, they encouraged her even more than they might have otherwise.

There's a big difference between a parent's expecting a child to achieve and encouraging him or her to learn.

Expecting a child to achieve places pressure on the child. The implication is this: If you achieve, your value increases, and if you don't achieve, it decreases. Invariably, a child's identity and self-esteem become linked to achievement. The net result is nearly always low self-esteem because few children ever see themselves as performing up to the standards their parents have set for them.

Encouraging a child to learn frees the child to do just that—explore, probe, test, and learn! This attitude separates a child's worth from his or her performance. It gives a child space to try out and try on various aspects of life. Value is a given. In an atmosphere of unconditional value, a child usually not only develops high self-esteem but also registers high achievement.

That's what happened to Joannie. She blossomed. In school, she gravitated toward friends who would encourage her, not push her. She gave her best effort to learning and made above-average grades. She developed strength in her convictions as well as very good communication skills. She developed a can-do attitude about life and learning. By the time Joannie graduated from junior college, she truly was not afraid to explore the unknown or try something new. She eventually became a stewardess on international flights and kept an apartment in New York City. Believe me, neither

Anne nor I could *ever* have anticipated that scaredy-cat Joannie would do that with her life!

No teacher made the difference in Joannie's life. Her peers certainly didn't; I among them. Her parents and other family members encouraged Joannie into becoming a good student.

In sharp contrast was my friend Cindy. Cindy's parents not only expected her to achieve, they demanded that she achieve at a specific and very high level. They continually prodded, bribed, and threatened Cindy to perform. Of course, they didn't think that's what they were doing. They thought they were *encouraging* their daughter. Their so-called encouragement was, in fact, unrealistic expectation.

All of Cindy's rewards and punishments were linked to her school performance. Her allowance was linked to grades on homework and quizzes, ice-cream cones were tied to test scores, her ability to attend slumber parties was linked to evaluation sheets from her piano teacher, and pretty hefty cash bonuses were given for straight A's.

Cindy's foremost concern all through school was with what she needed to do to get "a B or better." She wasn't really interested in learning, but only in doing what was necessary to keep her mom and dad off her back.

Although Cindy had a very high IQ and lots of natural talent, she hated school. She dreaded walking into the classroom from the playground, and she cared little for what her teachers had to say, other than in report cards and parent-teacher conferences. She became what we called a *boot shiner*. She did everything she could to manipulate teachers into giving her just a little bit more than she deserved in order to avoid criticism at home. And she was quite good at her craft.

Midway through her senior year in high school, Cindy left school. She had earned the bare minimum number of credits to graduate, and she never wanted to see a school again. Her parents were devastated, but Cindy was eighteen by then and of legal age to make her own choices. She left home and didn't return for three long years.

Cindy's teachers didn't turn her into a bad student. She arrived at school with all of the tendencies already in place to become a student who was disengaged, reliant on others, full of self-justification and blame for others, and incapable of sustained effort.

A Parent's Cry: "Why Me?"

After sharing my viewpoints with a friend, I wasn't at all prepared for her response. She rolled her eyes toward the sky and moaned, "Once again, it's all up to me. Why *me*?"

Up to that point, I hadn't realized how some parents might take their responsibility as their child's teacher as a heavy burden or as a setup for condemnation.

That is not at all my intention or my perspective.

I consider it a parent's *joy* to be a child's primary teacher, and it is a fairly easy role to fill if a parent is only willing to assume the responsibility.

How is it easy? We'll explore that in the next chapter.

Chapter 3

A Parent's Role as Teacher

When I was only an undergraduate college student, one of my education courses required that I tutor a student in a one-on-one setting. I was assigned to Ben, who needed help in reading.

The first evening that Ben arrived, I politely asked his mother the question we had been instructed to ask, "What is it that you are hoping Ben will accomplish during the next ten weeks?"

She replied tersely, "That he'll start getting an A in reading."

"An A?" I asked, to make certain I had understood her correctly. "What grade is he presently earning?"

"This last grade period he got a D," she said. "He's not doing well."

During this exchange, Ben was standing in his mother's shadow, head down, shoulders slumped, and cradling two small books in his arms. I have never seen a child appear more downhearted or embarrassed.

And then, to my surprise, Ben's mother sat down to watch me work with Ben. Not only was this not a part of the tutorial guidelines, but I knew that Mom's presence was exactly what Ben did not need. I politely suggested she go next door to the student union building for coffee or dessert while Ben and I worked. She replied, "Well, how will I know if Ben is reading better?"

I answered, "We probably won't know that, ma'am, for several weeks." Reluctantly, she withdrew.

I was overwhelmed. This mother wanted see her son's reading scores improve from a D to an A in twenty hours of tutorial time. Not only that, she wanted significant progress within the first hour! She was totally performance oriented. Oh, how I wished she had said, "I want Ben to be able to read better so he will know the enjoyment of reading and be able to explore all the wonderful books in the library." How I wished she had said, "I know my son is bright and capable of reading, but apparently something hasn't clicked into place for him. I'm hoping you can help." I would have preferred just about any goal other than better grades.

Before me sat Ben—only seven years old and already thinking of himself as a school failure.

I took the books from his hands and set them aside. I asked, "Ben, tell me a little bit about yourself. What do you like to do?"

Ben loved baseball and his puppy named Sloopy. He thought dinosaurs were cool. He liked to take care of his goldfish, and his favorite subject in school was math. "I'm pretty good at numbers," he told me. He also liked to work puzzles and informed me that he and his grandfather had almost completed a five-hundred-piece jigsaw puzzle. I was pretty impressed and told him so. Ben beamed.

I told him that I also liked baseball and that my dog's name was Hildie but that I'd never been very successful at keeping goldfish alive for longer than a few days at a time. He gave me a couple of tips.

Twenty minutes passed and we still hadn't cracked a book. Finally, I asked, "How do you feel about reading?"

Ben shrugged his shoulders. "I dunno. I'm not good at it."

"Any clues as to why reading is hard for you?" I asked.

"Nope," he said after a few seconds. "I'm just not good at it."

"Who told you that?" I asked.

"You heard my mom," he said. "I got a minus in reading."

"A minus?"

"Yeah," he explained. "The teachers give a student a plus or a minus for each subject. I got pluses in everything but reading. I got a minus in reading."

I was livid. There had been no D—and there would be no A! Ben's mother had created the grade levels herself.

"Have you ever thought of reading as a puzzle?" I asked Ben. "You know, like that jigsaw puzzle you are working with your grandfather."

"A puzzle?"

"Sure," I said. "Letters fit together to make a word just like pieces fit together to make a jigsaw. If you can work jigsaw puzzles, you can learn to put letters together into words."

"Really?" Ben brightened at the prospect.

"In fact," I went on, feeling very bold, "I bet you can already read." I wrote down the equation $2 + 2 = 4$. "What does that say?" I asked him.

"Two plus two equals four."

"You read that very well," I said, emphasizing the word *read.*

"Ah, that's not reading," Ben replied.

"Sure it is. Each one of those marks on the page stands for something you just read."

A light seemed to go on for Ben. "Yeah," he said. "I guess I can read."

And then I got very honest with Ben. "Ben, I'm not at all sure whether we can get all the way to an A in the next few weeks, but I'll promise you this: You're going to learn how to read. In fact, I think you're going to be a very good reader, and if I were a betting woman, I'd bet you're going to get a plus on your next reading evaluation."

Ben looked at me as if to say, "You really think so?" I smiled back and said, "Let's see if any of these books you brought are worth reading."

Half our session was gone by the time we finally opened a book. But Ben was relaxed and eager to see how reading might be a "puzzle."

When Ben's mother returned, I told her that the books she had brought were not the best ones. She needed to go with Ben to the library and find some second-grade level books on dinosaurs, fish, baseball, or dogs. She stared blankly at me, but two nights later, Ben showed up with a book on dinosaurs. We got to work and within a few weeks, Ben was reading everything in sight.

At the end of the ten-week session, Ben's mother said, "You've done wonders with Ben."

"No, *Ben* has done wonders," I replied. "Help Ben find books that are fun to read and that are about things he finds interesting. He'll be a lot more eager to practice his new reading skills. He's a very bright guy, and he's going to go far in school." I couldn't resist adding under my breath as she and Ben walked away, " . . . if you don't trip him up again."

Even though I was only a student myself, I knew enough to know that Ben's greatest obstacle to school success was likely to be his mother's high expectations about the grades she wanted him to earn.

In the last chapter we discussed briefly the difference between *expecting a child to achieve* and *encouraging a child to learn*. The child who is encouraged to learn experiences a great deal of freedom to explore new information.

The child who is sent off to school with the advice, "Learn all you can today so you'll be better able to explore the great, big, wonderful world awaiting you," is going to have a much better day at school than the child who is told, "Don't give your teacher any trouble, keep quiet—and you'd better get a good grade on that math quiz or no TV tonight."

In the same manner, the child who is greeted at the end of the day with the question, "What was the most interesting thing you learned at school today?" is going to have a lot more to tell his parent than the child who is asked, "What grade did you get on your history test?"

A Parent as a Co-Learner

A parent who adopts an "encourage to learn" approach to his child's education is also much more free!

If you are a parent who is performance-bound, you are going to feel as if you and your child are in a constant tug-of-war over grades and school assignments. On the other hand, if you shift your focus to being a co-learner and an encourager, you are likely to find that both you and your child have more joy related to schoolwork.

A parent once complained to me, "My son and I fight over his homework every night. I just can't get him to buckle down and do his assignments."

"Tell me what the homework routine is like in your house," I said.

"I insist that Josh go to his room and do his homework the minute he is finished with dinner. And then I come up to his room an hour or so later to check what he has done. I look over his papers. Most of the time, he has done hardly anything, and much of what he has done is wrong. Then we argue because I claim he isn't trying and he tells me that he is. We go round and round."

"Try a different approach," I suggested. "Say to your son this evening, 'Tonight, you get to be the mother. You give me your homework to do and I'll do it, and then you correct it.'"

"You want me to do his homework for him?" she asked incredulously.

"No," I said. "I want you to fill in the blanks on his homework pages with light pencil and then give him those pages to correct. Tell him that if your answer is right, he can write over your answer with bold dark pencil. If it's not right, he should change it to the right answer and tell you what you did wrong."

She came back to me a few days later with a big smile on her face. "I have been doing just what you said."

"And?" I asked.

"And, the first night, about halfway through the homework pages I realized that I didn't know how to work one of the problems. This new math really is new to me. I asked Josh to show me how to do it, and he did. A couple of nights later, I came across a problem I didn't understand fully. Josh didn't understand it either, so we looked up the information, and we did the problem together. Of course, as you probably intended for me to do, I made a couple of mistakes on purpose in one of those first assignments."

"Did Josh find them?" I asked.

"Right away," she said. "In fact, he seemed to take great delight in finding my mistakes."

"But overall, this has been a positive step?" I asked.

"Definitely," she said. "Probably the best thing that has happened in the last few nights is that I have come to see Josh in a very different light. I thought that because he was slack in doing his homework he wasn't trying or that he wasn't very smart. My thinking has really changed. Part of Josh's reluctance to do his homework apparently was that it was too *easy* for him most of the time, so it just seemed like busywork to him. And in one area, he didn't enjoy his homework because he didn't know what to do or how to go about getting the answers. Once we figured out where and how to do the assignments, he was off and flying."

Josh and his mother had become co-learners rather than warden Mom and prisoner Josh. Homework became an exercise in learning, not a task to accomplish.

I once gave a writing assignment in two different ways to college freshmen journalism students. To one class I said, "Write a five-page, double-spaced feature article on a topic of your choice. Do your best to follow all the journalistic guidelines and good writing principles we've discussed. It's due in four days."

To the second class I said, "I'm in the mood to learn something new. Teach me something you feel certain I don't know. I don't have a lot of time to read your papers so get right to the point. Please don't turn in more than five pages, double-spaced. But if you need to use a full five pages to give me the information about the subject, please do so. I'd like your papers in four days."

You can probably guess the result. In the first class, I got five-page papers, most of which were belabored and rather boring. Four of the students turned their papers in late.

In the second class, eighty percent of the papers were five pages in length; the remainder were four pages (with only one person turning in a one-page paper of "Hot New Jokes"—a very clever feature piece). The papers were very well done, and all of them were turned in on time.

I purposefully kept the papers until the students asked me when I was going to return them. It was four weeks before a member of the first class asked, "Are we ever going to get back our five-page feature articles?" Students in the second class started asking me the next morning if I had read their articles.

Which, do you suppose, were more likely to become enthusiastic, interesting, and hardworking newspaper feature writers? Those in the second class are better prepared to see their readers as curious to learn something they don't know.

If a parent says, "Teach me something that you've learned," the child is more likely to give an enthusiastic response than if the parent says, "Tell me what your teacher thought of your report." One approach encourages learning; the other requests a performance report.

Four Advantages Parents Have Over Schoolteachers

Parents can be encouraged by the fact that they have four major advantages that schoolteachers don't have.

First, parental teaching is rooted in the context of all of life.

A child sees what the parent teaches in the context of everyday life—not merely in the context of a schoolroom or a particular subject matter.

Take, for example, this lesson: *It's better to tell the truth than to lie.* A schoolteacher might present that lesson in the context of a unit about George Washington, who, as legend goes, was honest in admitting to the demise of a certain cherry tree. The lesson might come up again a few years later when a child studies the judicial branch of the United States government, learns to define the word *perjury,* and studies its consequences within the court system. Along the way, various teachers might relate the concept of lying to cheating and plagiarism or say to the student, "Don't lie to me about what happened on the playground."

Telling the truth is a daily matter in the home, however. It is not subject bound. Telling the truth is a very important thread in the fabric of all family relationships. Telling the truth builds trust, and trust is perhaps the most valuable of all hallmarks in creating a relationship that is stable and lasting.

Lying destroys trust. It eats away at the very essence of a relationship.

Who has the better opportunity to teach the lesson about lying—a parent or classroom teacher? A parent. Where is this lesson best taught—in the home or in the schoolroom? In the home. When and how is this lesson best taught—subjectively and on a daily basis, or objectively and periodically? Subjectively and daily.

Why? Because the lesson about lying has to do with all of life and is therefore best taught within the context of relationships that span all of life!

Take a look at this lesson about lying from a little different angle.

Consider Sally, who is taught to tell the truth at home. When Sally goes to school, she hears a teacher reinforce the importance of telling the truth. Is Sally more likely or less likely to tell the truth at school, having learned this lesson at home? More likely, of course.

Consider Frank, who sees and hears abundant lies at home and is never required in a consistent manner to tell the truth. When Frank goes to school and he hears a teacher insist that lying is wrong and telling the truth is always right, he has a very limited context for that lesson—the context of the school. Although the lesson is applicable to all of life, the conclusion Frank is likely to draw is that it is wrong to tell a lie in school. Frank has had very little life experience with the value of telling the truth. Is he more or less likely to tell the truth in school on a consistent basis? Less likely. Is he likely to carry this value of telling the truth back into his home? The answer is no.

What flows from the home to the school is much more potent and pervasive than what flows from the school to the home.

The example of telling the truth has to do with values. Of

course parents are better able to teach their children values. But the same applies to pure academics. Take a look at three examples that pertain to English, history, and science.

Several years ago, a young man in one of my speech classes spoke with impeccable grammar both in his formal presentations and in class discussions. I complimented Ken after class one day on his ability to use the English language and then I asked him, "Who taught you to speak with such precision?"

He blushed, grinned, and answered, "My grandmother."

"Was she a teacher?" I asked.

"No, just a grandmother," he said. "She took care of my sister and me after school for several years while we were children. She wouldn't let us use slang, and she always corrected us when we made grammatical errors."

"What happened if you made a grammatical mistake?" I asked.

"She'd say, 'There are lots of excuses for lots of things, but there's never any excuse for bad grammar,'" Ken replied, in a singsong manner that let me know he had heard that phrase often. "Grandmother believed that a person with good grammar could get any job he wanted and that, in order for a person to rise to the top of any field, he had to be able to speak well. She always told us that she wanted us to be able to go all the way to the top."

Ken took good grammar to school. What was taught to him by his English teachers only reinforced what he already knew and had learned was important.

Lindy came to college with a desire to be a history teacher. She was interested especially in the history of the Christian church. I asked her, "Where did you develop that interest? Did you have a good Sunday school teacher . . . a

"Was he a specialist in church history?"

"No. He was an accountant. But Uncle Martin loved to read about the early saints in the church and about important theologians down through the centuries. He always came to our house for holidays and my sister and I looked forward to Uncle Martin's stories. He could talk for hours. He knew all about every member of our family back through at least four generations, and he also told us stories about great men and women who were missionaries and founding church leaders. He really made those people come alive for us."

"What a wonderful privilege you had," I said.

"Yes," she replied. "I have great memories of listening to Uncle Martin. One of the things he said has really stuck with me all these years: 'Someday somebody will be telling someone about you. That's history. It's important they have something good to say.' "

Uncle Martin was not only a good history teacher; he was also an excellent philosopher. His niece developed a love for history far more from the context of her own home than from the schoolroom. In fact, when I asked Lindy if she had good history teachers, she said, "Some, I guess. But none of them was as interesting as Uncle Martin."

And then there was Andrea. It didn't take much effort to conclude that Andrea was a science major. She walked into my classroom for a show-and-tell speech with a butterfly net under one arm and a carousel of slides under the other. Andrea had been collecting and studying butterflies since she was a little girl. Her ambition was to establish a living collection of butterflies as part of a botanical garden or museum.

"Where did you get your interest in butterflies?" I asked.

"Mom gave me a book titled *The Girl of the Limberlost*,"

flies when we had science in school. I guess I've just always been fascinated by them."

"Did you have good science teachers?" I asked.

"My sixth grade science teacher was really good," she said. "He had a beetle collection. He taught me a lot about how to mount and preserve what I collected."

Andrea didn't gain a foothold on her life's work in school. She brought it to school, and school helped her further that interest.

Can parents and other family members influence the way a child approaches English, history, and science? You bet! Those interests developed within a whole-life context find specified application in school.

The converse can also happen, of course. What is said in a classroom may prick a child's interest and set him on the road to further discovery. It is the hope of every teacher, of course, that this happens.

But should that happen and the home not be supportive, the interest is likely *not* to grow. Several years ago, I met a man named Ted who at age thirty-eight had returned to college to pursue the degree he had always wanted: a baccalaureate in philosophy.

Ted had first expressed his interest in philosophy to his parents when he was a teenager. His father bluntly told him that philosophy wasn't practical and that he needed to study business or engineering. His mother warned him that such a major in college might turn him away from his faith in Jesus Christ. Ted majored in business management, went on to get an M.B.A., and became an investment banker. He was quite successful, but he still had a longing to study philosophy. And so, he went back to school.

and teaches all week. "I've never had so much fun," he said. "Aren't college students great?"

There's no way of knowing how many times a child has brought home an intriguing idea or academic dream only to have it crushed in the context of the home.

The whole-life context for learning is the edge parents have over teachers—for good or bad. A parent always needs to keep in mind that what happens in school can:

- enhance and reinforce what a child learns at home and
- spark an interest that a child will invariably test within the context of the home.

Second, parental teaching is grounded in a relationship that, ideally, is characterized by unconditional love.

Most children and young adults do not have a concept that their schoolteachers *love* them. Students may think their teachers accept or even admire them, but rarely do students feel that a teacher genuinely loves them unconditionally.

Love is very closely linked to two concepts: value and freedom. Psychologically healthy children know their parents value their presence on the earth and want them in the home, regardless of their personality or abilities. A parent has the high privilege of saying to his or her child, "I love you for who you are, not what you do." Every child needs to hear that from the parent. It's the most freeing, positive statement a parent can ever make.

Within a context of unconditional love, learning takes on a completely new meaning. A child sees learning as a means of fulfilling his or her potential as a person rather than fulfilling a parent's expectations.

tance of Sunday school lessons because they want their children to grow up to be capable and moral adults.

When love is the motivation for teaching, it also becomes the child's foundation for learning. A child who knows that he or she is loved unconditionally is:

- much more courageous in taking learning risks, including admitting that he or she doesn't have an answer or know certain information,
- more curious and creative, and
- more independent in his or her ability to solve problems, reach conclusions, make decisions, and conduct research.

Why? Because this child does not see school failures—be they poor grades or critical comments—as related to his or her value as a person. Thus, the child is more willing to take risks and try new methods. By contrast, the child who is loved for what he or she achieves is constantly weighing the risks associated with a new learning challenge.

As part of my undergraduate college experience, I helped teach a beginners' swimming class, most of whom were freshman. One eighteen-year-old woman said to me, "I can't get in water that deep because I'll drown."

"This water is three and a half feet deep and you are five feet four inches tall," I said. "That means that twenty-two inches of you will be out of the water. How can you drown if your head, neck, and shoulders are out of the water?"

"I just will," she said adamantly.

"Who taught you that?" I asked.

"My mother," she said. I finally convinced her to get into the pool but only after I jumped into the water and told her that she could hang on to me. We started with the very basics—putting her face into the water while she held onto my arms—but after several weeks, I not only had her swimming but jumping off a diving board into deep water.

"What exactly did your mother say to you about swimming?" I asked her at the end of the course. Her reply floored me.

"She said when I was just a little girl that if I got into deep water, I'd drown and then the county would take away my brothers and sisters. She told me that if I loved her and my brothers and sisters, I'd never go into water that deep."

Not only had this mother planted an unnecessary fear of the water in her child, but she had also tied that fear to family loyalty.

That case is extreme to be sure, but it is amazing how family love, or lack of it, determines a child's classroom performance.

A student once came to me in tears, saying, "I can't go home with these grades. My parents will disown me."

"Surely it isn't that serious," I said.

"It *is* that serious," she replied. "They told me just two weeks ago that if I didn't study hard enough to get a B average, I wasn't a child of theirs."

By contrast, I've also had students who were not high achievers but loved school because of great parental support.

One young woman named Rosie told me that her parents' advice had always been, "Go to college for at least a year, Rosie. It will be a great experience for you. You'll gain a lot that will help you all your life."

Rosie struggled with school. She had dyslexia that was not diagnosed until junior high. By then, she had learned to compensate for her disability to a degree, but she never made top grades and every class represented a new challenge to her. She had entered college on probation because her SAT scores were low and her grades marginal. When she came to me asking if she could take her exams orally because she had trouble taking written tests, I gladly complied.

I asked Rosie if her parents knew about her dyslexia. "Oh sure," she said. "They were the first ones to suspect I had a learning problem and they kept bugging the school officials until I was finally tested. My parents have never expected me to get the best grades in the world, but they have always encouraged me to find my own way of learning everything I can."

I have never seen prouder parents than Rosie's on the day she graduated from college. They were thrilled that their daughter had found her own way through college—with a low C average in grades but an A+ in zest for learning. Rosie had a built-in courage that directly manifested her parents' unconditional love for her.

I've known a number of Rosies in my life—students who were short on academic talent but long on thirst for knowledge. Without exception, they have had parents or some other significant family member who loved them for who they were and not for what they accomplished. And in all cases, they accomplished a great deal.

Therein lies the irony of the impact of love on learning. The more a parent gives a child freedom to learn, without pressure to perform, the more a child tends to learn—and in the process, the better the child performs. On the other hand, the more a parent insists that a child perform, the more suspicious of the school process the child tends to become, the less the child learns, and the poorer the child performs.

Again, it is the parent who provides this context of love to a child. A teacher may be able to provide a touch of love here and a tad of encouragement there. But it is from the home that a child draws the inner sense of value to say, "I believe I'm smart enough to learn this; but if I can't, I'm still valuable."

Third, parents can provide a far more consistent means of reinforcement than teachers.

Parents provide daily feedback to their children about who they are and what is or isn't appropriate behavior. In so doing, they give their children criteria for evaluating right from wrong.

They also provide lifelong feedback—well after any one teacher has come and gone in a child's life.

This combination of daily feedback and lifelong feedback is something parents can give and teachers cannot.

Parents need to understand that teachers spend far more time correcting their students than praising them. They give most exams to find out what students don't know so they can add instruction. On the whole, they spend more time with the worst students in class than with the best ones. This isn't the ideal, nor is it what most teachers would like. But it is the reality of the classroom format.

Furthermore, most students today—even at younger grade levels—have more than one teacher. Teachers specialize by grade and subject matter. In the process, a student is likely to have as many as seventy or more teachers by the time he or she gets out of high school.

This multitude of teachers can result in very mixed messages to a child about his or her performance as a student. A student may hear from a Spanish teacher, *"Muy bien.* You are doing very well," and the next hour hear, "I need to see you after algebra class to discuss this low test score." The student thinks, "I'm good at Spanish and lousy in algebra." What is the conclusion the student draws about himself as a person? Probably that he is pretty average—and, frankly, being average never inspired anybody.

Schools try to compensate for this multiplicity of teachers by providing guidance counselors and faculty advisors. The theory is that at least one trained educator will take an objective look at the whole of a student's performance and sort out strengths and weaknesses and help make wise choices about his or her academic future. More often than not, however, the student's advisor knows even less about him than any one teacher. In many cases, students see their advisors only long enough to have them sign their course schedules.

Who is the best advocate for the student, the most consistent observer of academic progress, and the richest source of rewards from learning? The parent!

These reinforcement functions happen best in the parent-child relationship because the parent has knowledge in three distinct areas that teachers don't:

1. The parent is able to see broader, long-range trends related to a child's performance.

"You're doing well in Spanish? I'm not surprised. You picked up French very quickly when that family from France moved into the neighborhood a few years ago. You seem to have a natural gift for languages. That's a wonderful skill to have."

"Trouble in algebra? That's a little strange, don't you think? You've always done very well in math here at home—and you're good at problem solving. Do you think maybe a tutor would help so you don't get off on the wrong foot in this area?"

The parent has a much better ability to see when a student does well under a particular style of teaching or has difficulty in a classroom organizational setting. Furthermore, a parent sees what a student chooses to study when he or she is not in school. The parent sees how patient the child is putting together a model airplane and how interested he or she is in books on flying. Thus, the parent is the one most likely to recognize the child's interest in aeronautics and will encourage that area of study.

2. The parent knows which rewards and punishments work best for the child.

Some children respond to grade reports; others don't. Some need a tangible expression of reward; others actually respond better to verbal praise. Teachers don't always know what motivates each child, and, even when they do, they're rarely able to get away from generalized reward and punishment methods. Therefore, everybody in the class gets a star for turning in a homework assignment, even though some children may find stars meaningless. And everybody gets a letter grade, even though some students might benefit more from a numerical score or a private evaluation.

The wise parent seeks both to encourage and reward effort. Very often, the most effective forms of reward and punishment are to praise highly those traits that are desired and to say nothing of those that aren't (as long as they don't cause harm to the student or others, of course). Rather than throw the book at the student who fails to try, parents should do their utmost to encourage effort and praise it highly. Children, like adults, love praise, and they pursue it.

3. The parent is more effective meting out rewards over time.

The reward methods of schooling change very little from first grade to graduate level. The parent knows when those methods need to change for he or she can see better what is happening in the child's life over time—what behavioral patterns seem to be forming, what influences seem to be growing and dominating, what relationships seem to be having the greatest impact.

In sum, the parent has the unique ability to say to a child, "Here's what I think," and to have that opinion grounded in years of observation and support, rather than a few weeks of highly structured association.

And the fourth advantage: Parents can teach children through daily modeling.

We all learn how to apply what we know by copying others. The pattern is this: We see a behavior. If it works for us, and we aren't hurt or punished in some way for doing it, we adopt it. If we see a way that we think is better, we try it. If it works for us, and we aren't punished for doing it, we change our behavior. In this way human behavior has been passed down for millennia. Teachers call the technique *modeling.* One person models a behavior that another person copies.

Paying attention ... speaking ... writing ... using tools ... planting seeds. These are all behaviors. We each learned *how* to do them by copying someone!

The best person for copying is the parent or guardian the child spends the greatest amount of time with *while trying out behaviors for the first time.* That's one of the reasons the first few years of a child's life are so critical to the learning process. That's when a child tries up to seventy percent of all the behaviors he or she will ever manifest, from walking to talking and beyond.

The person the child copies *first* is the most important person in the learning process. In other words, a person may not see another person manipulate a gauge on a nuclear reactor until he is thirty years old. The first person he sees manipulate that gauge is going to be the person he copies. On the other hand, if a child sees a parent brushing his teeth regularly, he might begin to copy that behavior at the age of two.

By the time a child enters school, he or she has already learned thousands of behaviors. The elementary school actually has very few new behaviors left to teach a child. What the elementary school does best is reinforce the behaviors a child has learned and then add information and specialized behaviors to the child's repertoire.

The school is not the best place for your child to learn how to sit still and concentrate. A child best learns that skill at home. And how? By copying a parent who sits still and focuses on a task.

A teacher is not the best person to teach your child how to respond to a question. Why? Because teachers ask more questions than they answer! The best place for a child to learn how to respond to a question is at home. And how? By copying a parent who listens to questions and responds to them patiently, thoughtfully, and eagerly.

A teacher is not the best person to teach a child how to follow directions. The best place for a child to learn that is in the home, by copying a parent who follows directions, gives directions, and supervises the way others follow them.

School functions best as an environment in which teachers direct the behaviors that a child has already learned into school tasks. The teacher can teach a child how to read but not if that child has no clue how small elements can be put together to make a whole; and not if the child has no desire to learn to read. The parent best shows a child that elements can be grouped together to make a whole—as in a jigsaw puzzle—and the parent best models reading by enjoying the newspaper or a novel. Parents are the ones who place value on reading by showing the many ways it is vital to making decisions in life.

A Natural Learning Context

In summary, then, parental teaching has these advantages over classroom teaching:

- a whole-life context

- a loving relationship
- the most effective means of reinforcement
- round-the-clock modeling

A better context, a more complete relationship, more effective reinforcement, and a more effective method—parents have a *superior* advantage over classroom teachers for virtually any behavior or any content they wish to impart to their children!

Those advantages still don't fully address, however, the concern of my friend who moaned, "Why me?" I suspect her dismay came from the fact that she didn't think herself qualified to teach her children because she wasn't formally trained.

But Andrea's parents didn't need teaching degrees to encourage their daughter to pursue a natural interest in butterflies.

Uncle Martin didn't employ a full-blown curriculum to teach his nieces about family and church history.

Ken's grandmother didn't need an English degree to teach her grandson good grammar.

Rosie's parents weren't trained to tutor their dyslexic daughter.

These parents and relatives all plied their talents as teachers within the normal flow of their lives. They didn't allocate time to be teachers. They simply and effectively and lovingly wove life's important lessons into the fabric of their days.

Teaching became a natural dimension of their parenting.

For centuries, the Jewish people have been regarded as among the best educated people on earth. The ancient Jewish method of education took place entirely in the home. In fact, not until fairly recently have the Jews had a community school system.

Children were expected to receive both moral and practical instruction in the home—to learn the praises of the Lord, a daily self-discipline, the history of God's people, the Law, occupational skills, and various strategies for self-defense. (See Deut. 6:20–25; 11:18–21; Ex. 19:6; 1 Sam. 16:7; Ps. 78:1–4; Prov. 13:24; 22:6, 15; 29:15; Isa. 28:9–10.) Instruction was oral for the most part. In nearly all respects, the instruction amounted to training—it was highly repetitive and behavior oriented.

Scriptures and tradition directed Jewish fathers to provide four things to their sons:

- *circumcision*—which included naming and blessing and, in generalized terms today, would be tantamount to providing an identity for a child.
- *an understanding of the Torah*—which included both the history of the people and God's laws for living.
- *a good wife*—a responsibility which, if applied to our culture today, might be considered the wisdom needed to choose a mate and friends and develop longstanding relationships.
- *a practical occupational skill*—the capability of earning a living with one's hands.

These instructional goals are not unlike those that parents face today. They can readily be generalized to apply to both sexes. It is the parent's primary responsibility to give their children an identity of belonging to a family and to a people. It is the parent's primary responsibility to teach a child the basics of the child's culture and traditions. It is the parent's primary responsibility to teach a child how to live in harmony with other people. It is the parent's responsibility to teach a child certain practical skills and the value of work. And all of these lessons flow naturally in the home as children copy the behavior of their parents, discuss life with them, and solve problems with their parents' help.

Deuteronomy 6:4–9 is the classic Scripture related to the parent's teaching role:

Hear, O Israel: The LORD our God, the LORD is one! You shall love the LORD your God with all your heart, with all your soul, and with all your strength. And these words which I command you today shall be in your heart. You shall teach them diligently to your children, and shall talk of them when you sit in your house, when you walk by the way, when you lie down, and when you rise up. You shall bind them as a sign on your hand, and they shall be as frontlets between your eyes. You shall write them on the doorposts of your house and on your gates.

In today's terms, the parent's classroom may be the dining table, the car, the mall, or any other place the parent and child visit together. It is crucial to instruct the child from morning to night, at work and at play. In this way, the child is given a perspective on the world at large. The home is to be steeped with life's instruction.

Yes, your child *can* become a good student under your tutelage. You as a parent are uniquely equipped and authorized to be your child's first and foremost teacher of the most important lessons in life.

What are those lessons you are best able to teach your child? What is the curriculum that needs to flow naturally and by example in your home? We turn our attention now to the twelve most important lessons *you* can teach your child.

Chapter 4

SIMPLE TRUTH

Lesson #1: You Are Never Alone

Through the years, I have had a number of conversations with college students who either had contemplated or attempted suicide during their earlier teenage years. Their reasons were expressed in various ways: "I didn't feel as if anybody understood what I was going through," or "I felt so alone," or "I didn't think anybody really cared whether I lived or died." Their suicidal tendency seemed born of a feeling of extreme isolation.

Keep in mind that this was the *feeling* I heard these students express, not the underlying thought or idea. The idea was generally, "I was going through a hard time," or "I had big problems," or "I was experimenting with alcohol and drugs."

In educational terms, the problem the student faced was the *content*, and isolation was the *feeling*. Both problems and feelings tend to be temporary. In all cases, the problem the student faced at age fifteen or sixteen was gone by nineteen or twenty. The students' feelings had changed, too. Perhaps that's why we often hear the expression, "Suicide is a permanent solution to a temporary problem."

Suicidal teens aren't the only ones who have problems or feel lonely. All teens go through bouts of feeling rejected or misunderstood. The truth is that *everybody* understands how it feels to face a problem alone.

Studies show that a child has felt every human emotion

by the time he or she enters elementary school! Fear . . .
rejection . . . joy . . . love . . . hope . . . anxiety. A toddler may
not be able to define these emotions, but he has felt them! The
ability to experience emotion has been given to us all.

The "Nobody" Statements

The cry "nobody understands" is one of four "nobody"
statements that are detrimental to a child. Let's take a look at
each one and the way it affects a child's development as a
student.

Nobody understands. Often a child or teenager will say,
"You just don't know." The person who makes this statement
is nearly always fearful and hurt. Something about life has
wounded the person, and he or she is retreating from the
problem.

In the classroom, the person who feels this way is nearly
always a student who doesn't understand the material or who
has failed to complete an assignment and is seeking justifica-
tion. "You just don't understand" becomes an academic excuse for either a failure to know or a failure to do.

When a student comes to me with this statement, my first
response is, "What is it that I don't understand? I'd like to.
Help me understand your situation."

The answer is usually one of the following.

"I'm under a lot of pressure" or "I have so many things
to do right now." The problem is one of time management.
These are problems that virtually all college students have, but
they are not unique to college. They can also be the plight of
a first-grader. The antidote is to take a serious look at the
student's schedule and time management skills.

"I'm having personal problems." These problems tend
to be *inter*personal, not personal, and nearly always involve
miscommunication. The answer is to take a long look at the

relationship that is causing the problem and seek some sort of resolution—either a break in the relationship or a reconciliation. This type of problem can strike a person at any age.

"I've been sick" or "I haven't been feeling well." A general sense of malaise can indicate a specific physical problem, which can affect a student's ability to learn. This problem might be a hearing or visual disorder. Again, this is a problem that is not unique to college.

"This is all new to me" or "I'm feeling overwhelmed by this course." This is probably due to a lack of study skills. The solution lies in determining what the missing elements are and whether the student needs remedial help.

What can you do as a parent to help your child when he or she says, "You just don't understand"?

First, don't attempt to convince your child that you do understand. Say that you would like to understand better, and ask for your child's help.

Second, attempt to sort out precisely what it is you aren't understanding. What is the underlying cause of the feeling of isolation?

Third, do your utmost to solve the problem. Provide the remedial help your child may need. Talk about relationship problems. Check out any physical symptoms that seem to linger. Help your child sort out his schedule. You may decide that someone else is in a better position to solve your child's problem or that it is unwise to solve it for him or her. In such a case, guide your child into making the decision or seeking assistance from others.

And finally, once the underlying problems have been addressed and solutions have started to take hold, talk about the feelings your child had. Help your child see that there was a difference between the feeling and the problems that were causing it.

Too often, a child is left alone in his feelings. When that

happens, the feelings tend to grow like weeds until they obliterate any hope of the child's ability to sort them out rationally.

That was the case with Patrick. I received notice that I was Pat's academic advisor only a week before two unsatisfactory midterm notices arrived from Pat's professors. I wasted no time in calling Pat and making an appointment with him.

Pat entered my office and brought with him a huge black cloud of despair. He was generally rumpled in appearance, and I noticed dark circles under his eyes. He spotted the unsatisfactory notices on my desk right away. "I'm trying to do better," he said defensively. "I've already been to see both of those professors."

"Oh, these?" I said, casually crumpling up the notices and tossing them into the wastepaper basket by my desk. "They aren't the problem."

"What is it, then?" he said.

"Those notices aren't the problem, Pat," I said. "They are just the warning flags—symptoms. Like a sore throat or a rash. My concern is not with these yellow slips of paper. My concern is for you. How are *you*? How are you feeling physically? How are you feeling about being in college? How are you feeling about life in general?"

"I'm all right," he said.

I didn't respond, hoping he would tell me more.

"I'm a little tired right now, I guess," he added after a few seconds.

"Tired physically or tired mentally or just sick and tired of everything?"

He smiled ever so faintly. "All of the above."

"It could be you've taken on too much this first semester. How many hours are you taking?" I asked.

"Eighteen."

"Eighteen?" I asked. "That's more than a full load. Why eighteen?"

"Well, I read in the catalog that a student could take up to eighteen hours without paying any extra, so I did. I figured out the total I needed, and I though by taking eighteen hours each semester and doing a couple of correspondence courses, I might be able to get through college a semester early and save my folks some money. I was a good student in high school so I thought I could do it without any problem."

"Tell me about your high school," I said. I learned in the next few minutes that Patrick, indeed, had been a good student in high school. He had a 3.8 high school grade point average. I also learned that he had gone to a small rural school with only eighty-three people in the entire high school. Pat had taken solid academic subjects for the most part but nothing that might have been considered an honors course. His hometown, about five hundred miles from campus, was a small farming community. The entire town equalled one third the population of the college's student body.

"Do you find college harder than high school?" I asked.

"A little. It's different. I think my main problem is that my roommate just doesn't understand that I need to study. Neither do any of the other guys on my floor."

"Tell me about them," I said. Pat's roommate was a physical education major and a member of the college baseball team. He was taking twelve hours, mostly physical education and recreation courses. Pat was living on a floor that housed most of the baseball team. His roommate and friends had little interest in studying and were taking courses that didn't demand a great deal of study. Pat, by comparison, was taking heavy-duty courses and too many of them.

Pat was also angry. He described the floor's party atmosphere, the constant, loud music in the dorm, and the frequency of his roommate's interruptions. He was carrying a big load of resentment and frustration.

"No wonder you're tired," I said. "You may think your

roommate doesn't understand, but let me assure you that I do. I understand that you are in a situation that has too many pressures and not enough time or space."

Together Pat and I mapped out a plan that included an immediate move to a different floor of the dorm, the dropping of one course, and tutorial sessions for the two courses in which he was performing poorly. We went over his daily schedule and blocked out eating and sleeping times to be kept regardless of whether homework was done. "If you don't have physical energy, you aren't going to have mental energy," I noted.

Five weeks later Pat stopped by the office. I hardly recognized him when he walked in. His posture was erect, he had a smile on his face, his shirt was neatly pressed, and his hair was combed stylishly. "I came to say thanks," he said shyly.

"Sit down for a few minutes and tell me how you are doing," I said.

"I'm passing everything. I've made some new friends who study as much as I do. I feel a lot more together than I did a few weeks ago."

"Good," I said. "You've got all it takes to be a successful college student, Pat."

Then Pat asked, "Why couldn't I see what was happening? Changing dorm rooms and dropping a class was really simple. But I just didn't see it."

When a student becomes overwhelmed by a problem to the point that physical exhaustion sets in and bitterness takes root, he can rarely see his way out of the problem by himself. He simply concludes that "nobody understands" and retreats further into the isolation of his feelings.

Help your child learn to disassociate feelings and problems and to tackle problems first. As problems are resolved, the negative feelings attached to them tend to evaporate. On the other hand, if you focus on feelings, your child is likely to become more and more defensive—and rightly so. Your child's feelings are his or her own. They're real. The more entrenched the feelings become, the less able your child will be to see problems. The cycle can become one of despair.

Listen closely to your child if he or she tells you he isn't "feeling" very good about a particular course or teacher. Probe that feeling. Search out the underlying issue. We rarely feel bad without a cause.

Nobody cares. On the surface, "nobody cares" may seem like "nobody understands." But they're different. The child who says, "You don't care," is really saying, "You don't care about what *I* want or that what *I* think is important."

Every person is self-centered to some extent. If our desires are thwarted, we tend to think other people are being uncaring. The fact is that those who say "no" or "later" to us probably care a great deal—so much so that they have laid boundaries to protect us from something harmful.

The way to respond to "nobody cares" depends on whether your child is mad or sad.

If your child is angry or upset, give him an opportunity to cool off. Say gently, "I may not care as much as you think I should, but I care enough to talk about this further." Set a time in the not too distant future for a one-to-one powwow, and then keep that appointment.

If your child is more sad than angry, take time right away to sit down with him and say, "You may be right. I may not have been caring enough. What is it that you really want?"

Your child's answer is likely to be something trivial—a piece of candy, a toy, time to play with a friend, the privilege to stay up later. Listen and weigh your child's request. In some cases, the desire may be legitimate.

Then assure your child of this: "You have told me what you want. Let me tell you what I want. I want you to grow up to be a healthy person who is an eager learner and able to relate to other people in a loving way. I am responsible as a parent for seeing that you become such a person. I want you to be such a person because I believe that you will have more joy and success in your life if you are healthy, always learning, and always loving. Now, what we need to figure out is how what you want relates to your being more healthy, a more eager learner, or a more loving person."

Such a speech may sound like a long answer to a child, but too often parents give their children answers that are too short. Give your child something to think about!

Ultimately life is a series of compromises with other people. No one gets what he wants all the time. By your quiet, controlled conversation, you are showing your child that compromise is not a power struggle or a time for yelling or threatening, nor does compromise result only in loss.

Don't be surprised if the main thing your child wants, after all, is your time and attention. The real cry may be, "I want more of you. I want to see you more, be with you more."

That's a legitimate want, and the only way to satisfy it is with your presence. Your child needs not only quality time with you but quantities of time. If your child is truly going to know that you care, he or she needs to know that you are available to listen, observe, and respond when he has needs.

A student named Gloria once said to me about another professor, "He doesn't care about us students."

"What is it that you want from him that you aren't getting?" I asked.

"What are you saying?" she asked.

"Well, when we say that somebody doesn't care, we're usually saying that he isn't meeting some need we have. What do you wish this person would do for you? What do you want him to do?"

"I want him to know my name," she said. "I want him to be able to say *Gloria* when he calls on me in class."

Through the years I have found that students define a professor's level of concern in a number of ways:

- "I want him to keep his office hours so I can stop by and see him."
- "I want him to keep the appointments he makes with me."
- "I wish she would take time to talk to us after class."
- "I would really like it if he recognized me when he saw me in the cafeteria. He seems to look right through me."
- "I'd like it if just once she asked a question about me instead of always talking about what she wants. She gives me a lot of advice but never seems to notice that I haven't asked for it."

Children tend to feel the same way about their teachers as they do their parents. They want parents and teachers alike to be present, not absent; to recognize them, not ignore them; to spend as much time listening as they do talking; and in general to count them as being important. They want their teachers and parents to want what *they* wanted as children: a two-way relationship.

How can you as a parent help build a basic quid pro quo relationship with your child in a way that is helpful to his ability to learn?

First, give your child options. Rather than say, "You can't do A, B, and C," let your child know he or she can choose between X, Y, and Z. These options (obviously they need to be age appropriate) can include food choices, play choices, or the choice of which subject to study first. A child who is given options has an opportunity to exercise his or her own will.

Second, insist that your child follow through on his choices. A child needs to learn that his or her choices have consequences. If he opts for a sweet snack rather than dessert, he should not be given dessert, too. If he wants to watch a particular program, he should watch it all rather than switch channels five times. If he wants to take lessons in a particular area, he should commit to taking them for a specified period of time.

Third, whenever possible or appropriate, give your child reasons for the decisions you make. Let your child see by your own behavior that you are a reasonable, rational person who bases decisions upon facts. Talk to your child about your own decision-making process. Let her know how you came to certain conclusions—such as what led you to your opinion that children under age twelve should not watch PG-13 movies or that a nine-year-old should be in bed by nine o'clock each school night.

Fourth, make yourself available to your child. In academe, professors often speak of having an open-door policy to students. This generally means that they keep certain hours in their offices with the doors open, and students can feel free to drop in at any time. Ask yourself, *Is there a time and place in each day where my children know I am available to them? Do they feel free to come and go from me with their concerns?*

In addition to an open-door policy, have an open-heart-and-mind policy. Are you willing to let your child speak freely about what he thinks and feels? Are you available to hear *anything* your child wishes to tell you? How have you expressed that willingness to your child? It is not enough to say, "You can come to me at any time." Your child needs to know that you truly desire him or her to come and be with you—just to spend time together without regard to a particular agenda.

Nobody wants me. The person who says "nobody understands" and "nobody cares" is likely to take a further step and conclude, "nobody wants me." He believes nobody wants what he has to give. Variations on the theme include "nobody likes me" and "nobody wants to be my friend."

In most cases, a person who believes that "nobody likes me" must first be assured that he or she has something worth giving to others and then must be taught how to find those who will appreciate it.

A number of years ago I had a young man named Larry in one of my communication classes. I noticed after a couple of weeks that Larry always sat in the back corner of the room. Often he left a seat between himself and the person closest to him.

Early in each semester I try to invite each of my classes to my home for a social gathering—in part, so I can get to know them better and in part, so they can get to know each other better. Most of the students are freshmen and sophomores living many miles away from their homes, so they welcome an opportunity to make new friends.

As I roamed from room to room with a tray of snacks during one such gathering, I found Larry alone in the sunroom reading a magazine. "What are you reading?" I asked.

He looked up in surprise. "Oh, *Time* magazine." I recognized from the cover that the issue was several weeks old and quickly concluded that Larry was hiding out.

"You're disappointing all the cute girls in the kitchen," I said, trying hard to be upbeat and social.

"Yeah, sure," he said, blushing.

I went back to into the kitchen and said to a small group of girls who were slicing cheese onto crackers. "Why don't you see if you can't make Larry's day. He's sitting in the sunroom reading a magazine."

"Larry?" one girl asked. "He's hard to impress."

A second girl added, "He's a strange one."

Another girl joined in. "Yeah, a group of us tried to talk him into joining us for lunch last week and he totally blew us off. I don't think he'd be very happy if we interrupted him while he's reading."

Larry left a short time later.

Over the next couple of weeks I watched Larry and came to the conclusion that he wasn't a snob or antisocial. He simply was shy. I went to the student cafeteria a few days later, and when I spotted him eating alone, I asked him if I could join him. He agreed reluctantly.

"Tell me a little bit about yourself, Larry," I said. "I don't feel as if I know you very well, and I'd like to get better acquainted."

Getting Larry to talk was like pulling teeth. I finally learned that he was an only child born to older parents. He had always loved to read, especially science magazines and books. He was a biology major and hoped to go into research or pathology. I asked him if he was a member of the premed club or the science honor society. He wasn't.

Finally I asked, "Larry, what's the wildest thing you've read about in your science books lately? What's the strangest or most awesome thing you've learned?"

Larry proceeded to tell me about a television program that he had seen about a farmer in California who was raising and selling snails as an alternative form of protein for the American diet. This was hardly a topic I cared to think about over lunch, but I forced myself to listen intently and to ask questions.

The more Larry shared, the more animated he became and the more expansive our conversation became. He covered several more "recent discoveries." By the time lunch was over I could say to him genuinely, "Larry, this has been one of the most enjoyable and informative lunch hours I've ever spent in this cafeteria." Larry smiled and replied, "Any time."

"You need to be in one of the science clubs. You have a lot to offer the other students." Almost as a whim I added,

"You might want to consider coming to a meeting of the student newspaper staff. We're always looking for new writers. We've never had a science column as far as I know. You'd be a great person to write that."

To my surprise, Larry showed up at the next student newspaper recruiting session. He submitted a feature story, the student editors responded to it, and before the year was out, Larry had a regular column in the paper and had made quite a circle of friends as a result. His columns always bordered on the quirky and obtuse—some remote facet of biology or chemistry—but they were always very cleverly written. Larry turned "being weird" into being charming.

He was a prime example of a student needing first to see that he had something worthy to be shared and then finding an avenue for sharing it.

What can you do to help your child find a niche in his or her world?

First, help your child see that he has distinctive inner gifts to offer others. Those gifts might include:

- something he knows that others don't know
- a smile
- a willing heart and hands eager to help out
- a skill or talent
- an ability to lead or organize
- an interest or hobby
- a listening ear

Be aware that a child tends to think in concrete terms. To a child, a *gift* might easily be construed to be candy. Emphasize to your child that he or she is a treasure chest of inner gifts that never run out. The more a person gives them away, the more he or she is filled up on the inside. Inner gifts grow the more they are given.

Second, help your child find people who will appreciate receiving. Teach your child early that not everybody likes everybody else equally. People have different personalities and talents, so we "fit" better with some people than others. This has nothing to do with gender, age, race, or nationality. It has to do with *personality*.

One of the most effective ways to share this concept with young children is to show them pieces of a puzzle. Children readily understand that certain pieces go together while others do not. The goal in terms of human relations, of course, is to find those people with whom you have the most in common—or who need what you have to give and who have to give what you need the most.

Help your child see that no one person is going to fit with him *exactly*. At the same time, he can nearly always find *something* in common with just about everybody.

A student once shared this bit of wisdom she learned from her grandmother: "Find your song, and then find an audience that wants to hear it."

Help your child find ways that are appropriate to give. Giving involves not only the gift but knowing when and how to give it. Here is where parental modeling is especially important.

There's a time, place, and method for giving what we have to give. We give best when . . .

. . . the other person is ready to receive. This can be taught in very concrete ways. For example, don't let your child interrupt others when they're talking. A person can't listen and talk at the same time. Teach your child that other people are better able to receive the gift of what he has to say when they're in a listening mode not a talking mode.

. . . we're expecting nothing in return. The person who gives in order to receive is manipulative. Don't let your child tie strings to the inner gifts he gives. He shouldn't expect a reward for listening, lending, or sharing.

. . . we give generously and spontaneously. Teach your child to be on the constant lookout for need. That's one of the greatest ways to help your child become less self-absorbed and be more outgoing.

Knowing that you have something worth giving is a matter of self-esteem. Knowing when and how to give your gifts is a matter of manners and propriety. The former is instilled when you express gratitude for your child's presence. The latter is taught as you train your child in appropriate behaviors.

Nobody else is involved. This belief is often stated in terms of "I'm not hurting anybody else," or "Nobody else needs to know," or "This doesn't involve anybody else."

The reality is, however, that John Donne was right when he wrote:

> No man is an island entire of itself; every man is a piece of the continent, a part of the main. If a clod be washed away by the sea, Europe is the less, as well as if a promontory were, as well as if a manor of thy friend's or of thine own were. Any man's death diminishes me, because I am involved in mankind, and therefore never send to know for whom the bell tolls; it tolls for thee (*Meditation*, XVII).

How can you help your child be part of the whole?

First, don't allow your child to become intellectually arrogant. Your child may have a higher IQ than another child, better grades, or better school skills. Teach your child that his or her ability to learn is a precious gift. Applaud your child's achievements. Help your child acquire study, memorization, and reasoning skills. But do not allow your child to see him or herself as superior to others on the basis of intellect. This type of arrogance ends friendships and brings great personal misery.

Second, insist that your child communicate with you. This doesn't mean you have to have a blow-by-blow account of all his feelings. I once overheard a child say to his mother, "I haven't thought up a new thought yet!" Nor does this mean forcing your child to talk. Don't manipulate or demand that your child converse with you. Rather, set a climate and make time for your child to talk to you in a way that is free-flowing. There should be no subject that is off limits.

From the day your child begins to talk, insist that he or she talk to *you* as well as to others in your family. Draw out your child's opinions and feelings. Encourage him to be disclosing and truthful.

When you insist that your child communicate with you at early ages, communication becomes a natural part of your relationship. Your child is much more likely to communicate with you openly as a teenager and as an adult.

"But," you may say, "isn't this an invasion of my child's right to privacy? Shouldn't I give my child all the time and space he needs to become his own person intellectually?"

Insisting that your child communicate is not an invasion of privacy but an exercise in helping him learn how to reason and communicate ideas. Communication about feelings forces your child to vent anger before it builds into seething rage. It also helps your child learn to identify and define feelings.

Your child will be healthier psychologically and intellectually by being required to communicate, and regular communication will give you greater insight into what is happening in your child's life. You'll be able to evaluate mood swings and diagnose problems earlier—physical, emotional, learning, relational, or spiritual. Overall, you'll have a much better understanding of your child as a unique and valuable creation of God.

Third, be your child's best listener. Answer your child's questions as fully as possible. If you don't have time to answer or need more information, let your child know you would like to discuss it later—and then make certain you do.

Don't dismiss your child's comments as trivial. In fact, don't ascribe any labels at all to your child's communication.

Ask questions, but don't interrogate. Express honest interest, but don't gush. Give opinions, but do so sparingly. Allow silence to communicate, too. Don't insist that every minute be crammed with words, but enjoy sharing moments together in stillness.

Communicating with your child in this manner is the best possible way to express, "You are a vital part of my life and this family. None of us in this family operates alone. We need each other."

In school, your child will be asked often to express his ideas and opinions: in one-on-one conversations with a teacher, in small group exercises, in presentations before an entire class, and in writing. The child who comes to school able and willing to talk with the family is well prepared for classroom communication. Such a child knows that ideas are meant to be shared. They are not intended to be the sole possession of any one person.

Building an "Everybody" Approach to Learning

This chapter has addressed the "nobody" arguments that children and young adults frequently voice. You can also instill in your child an "everybody" perspective—an approach to life and learning that includes others.

Have family conversations. When I was a child, our family breakfast table was the place to map out the day ahead. Each family member knew fairly well what the others had scheduled. The dinner table was the place to debrief what had happened during the day. Most nights we shared opinions freely and a sense of closure was brought to the day.

You may not have the luxury of being able to gather your entire family together for two complete meals a day. But if at all possible, carve out a specified time and place each day for the mutual sharing of ideas. Ideally every family member should have access to every other family member during those times.

Try turning off the television set to make some evening time available for conversation. Let the exchange flow naturally and freely. The day's events will probably be agenda enough for covering most of life's important topics during any one month.

Travel by car can be another opportunity to communicate. Structure your vacations to include time together for talking.

Don't declare any topic or subject off limits. Do control your own opinions and temper. Rather than debate an idea, ask your child to give reasons for the opinions he or she holds. Encourage your child to explore other avenues of reasoning. Don't expect your child to parrot your own ideas or agree with you on everything.

Spend time with your child. In our hurry-up-and-go world we often think that a few minutes a day of quality time is sufficient to spend with our children. A child also needs quantity time—knowing that Mom or Dad is available on the child's terms. A child's terms, of course, tend to be *when needed.* There's no guessing precisely when a parent is going to be needed—when the bicycle crash may occur or a fight break out. Therefore, as much as possible and especially when your children are young, do the utmost to be available as many hours in a day as possible.

If both parents are working outside the home, that availability may have to be by phone. If at all possible, have a private line or carry a cellular phone for just those moments. Your child will feel as if he is in touch, and you won't need to worry about tying up a company phone line.

Let family take priority during off-hours and weekends. There's no substitute for spending time together in creating an "everybody" identity for your child.

Assign your child family-related chores. Most parents require their children to keep their rooms clean, to pick up their clothes, and so forth. It is also important, as soon as your child is old enough, for him to have simple family-related chores. These include emptying the wastepaper baskets, loading the dishwasher, setting the dinner table, helping with the cooking (even a task as simple as tearing up lettuce for the salad), changing beds, raking leaves, weeding flower beds—nothing beyond the child's physical ability and certainly nothing that requires dawn-to-dusk labor. Group-related chores are important in helping your child see that he or she is a vital member of the group and that without his or her effort, the group is less able to function. In the process, you are equipping your child with general life skills.

Attend your child's school functions and extracurricular performances. Be your child's best fan. Your child should be able to count on you to applaud his successes and dry his tears of disappointment. Don't insist that your child "win." Be there in a supportive role simply because your child is your child.

Give your child ample opportunity to participate in group activities. My own childhood was filled with groups of various sizes and purposes: art class, Camp Fire Girls, swimming lessons, piano lessons, vacation Bible school. My brother traded Camp Fire Girls for Boy Scouts, Little League for art class, and saxophone lessons for piano. These group activities were fairly evenly spaced in any given week, month, or year.

We both had lots of playtime with friends in our home or yard. These groups exposed both of us to many different types of people, including those of races and cultures that were not our own.

Some of your child's groups should be structured; others should be unstructured or social. Some of the groups should have a range of ages, including a few children one to three years older and a few children one to three years younger. The groups should be of varying sizes—most should range from two to twenty members. Some of the groups may be short-term, others might last for years.

Place an emphasis on cooperative groups. If competition is involved, it should be group competition involving team play.

My doctoral research focused on the value of small groups in imparting information. The evidence clearly showed a highly significant correlation between small groups and an enhanced ability to learn new information, especially when a person was a new member of a group or the group was newly formed. Old-timers in an environment or group, by contrast, learned better in a lecture or self-study mode.

That is not the way schooling is structured. Lecture is still the basic way students—both young and old—are introduced to new information, whether it's math class in first grade or History 101 in college. Small groups are de rigueur for students studying specialized information, such as that in upper division college courses or graduate schools. The more effective way, however, appears to be just the opposite. People benefit more from small groups and peer interaction in *initial* learning.

For this reason it is very important for your child to interact in lots of groups, in order to be exposed to the many aspects of his or her culture. To a great extent, your child's self-esteem will be created by the groups where your child feels he belongs as a fully accepted member, the first and foremost of which is your own family.

As a parent, exercise your right to choose your child's groups. Don't leave peer selection to your child, but put your child into groups that support your family values and beliefs.

This doesn't mean finding groups of the same race, nationality, or socioeconomic level. It does mean finding groups that are mostly the same culture. Place your emphasis on similarities that span racial and economic differences.

If you find that your child is not accepted by a group or is making associations that result in frequent misbehavior, put an end to that group affiliation. There are lots of groups to choose from. Find the ones that bring the most benefit to your child.

Teach your child how to be a good group member:

- to show respect for others in the group, giving them ample opportunity to share the spotlight
- to see value in others of differing race, gender, age, religion, nationality, or ethnicity
- to applaud others in the group, cheering them on to individual and group success
- to do his part in the tasks or work of the group, whether helping put up the tent or cleaning up after the party
- to show respect to a group leader
- to speak up and offer suggestions for the betterment of the group

Group involvement gives your child a sense of belonging and teaches about the rights and responsibilities of membership. Children who are exposed to a variety of groups tend to be better problem solvers and have more realistic, open-minded thinking. Their language skills are better, and they tend to be able to discern outcomes and trends related to group processes.

Your Child Is "Somebody"

The child who sees that everybody has importance and that he is never fully alone or isolated is a child who has a growing sense that he is somebody—and in particular, somebody important within a group.

The child who has favorable group membership is a child who comes to see that groups are generally supportive, helpful, and informative. This perception readily transfers to school, which is for the most part a group activity. It also prepares your child to live in a family and neighborhood of his own one day.

Chapter **5**

SIMPLE TRUTH

Lesson #2: Ask!

Questions are at the very heart of education.

We do not learn unless we *want* to learn. The "want to" of learning comes because our curiosity is pricked. We first must see, hear, smell, taste, touch, or sense something we do not understand and which evokes our curiosity. When the moment comes that we want to learn, we begin asking questions. The more astute our questions, the more accurate and beneficial the answers will be. Asking questions and receiving answers is the process of schooling.

Have you ever seen a group of children watching a magic show? They usually sit wide-eyed and open-mouthed, in rapt attention. As soon as the magician has worked his tricks, the questions tumble out: "How did you do that?" "Was that person really cut into two pieces?" "Will you show me how to do that?" "Where did that rabbit come from?"

Oh, that teachers would learn a little from magicians!

I once had such a teacher. He always walked into the classroom exactly two minutes before the bell and wrote a sentence on the chalkboard. Then he sat down and folded his hands wordlessly until one of us asked a question or made a comment. The first class session, we sat in silence for almost ten minutes before one student asked, "What's going on?" Most of the time, this professor answered questions with questions of his own. He rarely tried to present definitive answers even though this was a history class. He never lectured and would not give his opinion unless a student asked him directly, "Professor, what do you think about this?" or "Professor, why did you write that on the board?" At heart, this man was a magician—using the "trick" of a statement to provoke his students into thinking and responding.

Two sayings have been passed down through the ages:

- It is better to know some of the questions than all of the answers.
- To get the right answers, you need to ask the right questions.

Few Answers, Many Questions

Without a doubt, no one knows everything, no matter how old or experienced he may be. Furthermore, no one person knows everything needed to make it through life with the bare minimum of problems and the maximum rewards.

The person who thinks he knows it all ... doesn't. Such a person is arrogant, not brilliant. But this arrogance is common in the college classroom, where some students routinely attempt to correct other students.

Nancy was such a student. She always came to class having read the prescribed lesson. She was also well-read, up on current events, a world traveler, and had enjoyed numerous privileges as a child in terms of lessons and cultural experiences. In other words, she was an intelligent person.

If another student made an error in class, however, Nancy was quick to point it out. She rarely missed an opportunity to present the right answer or to insist that other students hold the right opinions or make the right decisions.

The natural tendency of a teacher with a know-it-all

student is to try to bring the student down a peg by showing up some area of inaccuracy or fault in their comments. I was a fairly young teacher at the time I had Nancy in my college writing class, but I realized that making such comments would be unfair and counterproductive to Nancy and in the long run would not be a good example to the rest of the class.

Still, I could see other students becoming discouraged and frustrated with Nancy's attitude. The day I overheard one of the other students in a whisper refer to Nancy as *Miss Smarty Pants*—a phrase I hadn't heard since grade school—I decided to have lunch with Nancy. Something had to be done to change the mood of hostility that was growing in the class.

After we had eaten and talked about general subjects for nearly an hour, I asked Nancy if she would tell me a little about her family. I told her I was curious as to what kind of parents had produced such a good student. She spoke of both her mother and father in glowing terms. They were educated, loving parents who had provided a wonderful childhood for her.

"Did they place a lot of demands on you?" I asked.

Nancy hesitated and dropped her eyes. "Nothing that wasn't good for us." I detected a small chink in the armor.

I responded in as lighthearted a manner as I could muster. "That sounds to me like a childhood with lots of hours of practice, practice, practice."

She simply said, "Yes."

"Were you and your brother and sister allowed to ask a lot of questions?" I asked.

"No. There wasn't much opportunity for questions."

"Nancy," I said, "I've been thinking about making an assignment to the class. Let me try it out on you. You are so aware of things in our culture . . . of all the books you have read and movies you have seen, what situation or anecdote from literature best describes your own growing up years?"

She thought for a few moments and then said, "Have you seen the movie *The Sound of Music*?"

"Yes."

"Do you recall the relationship that the father had with his children prior to Maria showing up as their governess?" I quickly thought back over how the widowed Captain von Trapp had operated like a drill sergeant with his children, demanding perfection and precision from even the youngest child.

"That was the atmosphere of our home. Dad didn't have a whistle, but that's about the only difference."

"And Mom?"

"She was more like one of us children."

"So your father was concerned that you always behaved correctly, had all the right answers, and responded in the right ways?"

"Always."

Dear Nancy. Her home had been overwhelmingly top-heavy with answers, and all of the communication that had flowed from parent to child was laden with directives. No wonder Nancy was so concerned with getting it right.

"In my experience, Nancy," I said, "there are very few right answers that work for everybody in all situations. Those few answers are certainly worth having, but they tend to involve the big issues of life, not the day-to-day workings."

In typical Nancy fashion, she responded, "I know that." And then she added, realizing perhaps that she had inadvertently wandered into something of a trap, "But it's hard for a person who is conditioned to give only right answers to admit to being wrong."

She was right as usual. It's *very* hard for a child who is forced to be right ever to admit that he is wrong. But all children are wrong from time to time. They know it, and others know it. An inability to admit mistakes results in denial, resentment, and alienation. Such a child rarely knows how to forgive others—or receive forgiveness himself. The child will end up alone and miserable unless someone meaningful to the child in later years gives "permission" to be wrong and still be loved. Changing this mind-set takes a great deal of time and effort, both on the part of the observer and the person who is attempting to change a deeply ingrained response.

As a parent, you are in the best possible position to teach your child the following important lessons about being right:

- People see things differently. There are very few clear-cut, black-and-white, right-and-wrong conclusions about life.
- Most "right answers" relate to history and to concrete mechanisms or formulas, not to people's lives or opinions.
- To be wrong occasionally is human.
- Admitting a wrong is good. That is the first step toward correcting an error.
- Very few mistakes are irreversible. While we should try to avoid making mistakes, the more important lesson is to learn how to remedy the mistakes we make.
- Asking good questions is the remedy for being wrong so we can learn the better way; and if we hurt someone in being wrong, we must ask for forgiveness.

How might you instill these lessons in your child? There are nine natural, unstructured ways.

1. Never require your child to be perfect in order to be loved. Let your child know without a doubt that he is loved even when he makes mistakes.

This does not mean taking your child's mistakes lightly or letting grievous errors go unpunished. It does mean being very careful in determining what warrants punishment. Accidents happen. Everybody makes innocent errors in judgment—intending to do the right thing but somehow failing. These accidents and errors should never be punished. They do need to be pointed out and discussed. But mistakes are a part of being human.

Willful acts of disobedience, on the other hand, need disciplinary action. If your child makes a decision to act in a way that harms herself, other people, or property, she should be dealt with. Discipline should always be tied to the offending behavior in as concrete a way as possible so that the child truly sees a connection between what she did and the consequences she must suffer. If she takes the family car without permission, for example, she should lose driving privileges for a time. If a child hits a sibling, he should not be allowed to play with that sibling or that sibling's toys for as long as it takes for true repentance to set in.

In no way, however, should either willful acts of misbehavior or accidental mistakes be linked to a parent's love. A parent should never say, "I will disown you if you . . ." or "You are not my child if you . . . " Such ultimatums do not make a child better behaved or perfect.

2. Avoid setting standards that are impossible for a child to reach. I have never met an adult who went through childhood without having at least one skinned knee, one black eye, or one torn garment.

3. Don't correct your child in public or allow the child to correct his siblings publicly. Shaming your child is not good discipline. Wait until you are alone to tell your child why you want him to be able to tell a story properly or give directions accurately. Your child should show the same respect to his brothers and sisters. If he is allowed to interrupt them, he learns that it is okay to be impolite. He also develops a pattern of intellectual one-upmanship. Such behavior is rooted in issues of personal power, not a genuine desire for accuracy.

4. Insist that your child apologize when his mistakes or willful misbehavior causes harm to others. Require your child to make restitution for damages he may have caused.

5. Let your child know you don't know everything. Life has mystery. God is mysterious. We can't have all the answers because life has an eternal dimension to it and we're locked in time.

But we can seek wisdom—the full application of God's principles and purposes to life's facts. Teach your child what the book of James says about wisdom.

> If any of you lacks wisdom, let him ask of God, who gives to all liberally and without reproach, and it will be given to him. But let him ask in faith, with no doubting (1:5–6).

What a wonderful lesson to teach your child! God gives wisdom generously, and He never ridicules anyone for asking.

6. Always answer your child's questions fully, with a spirit of generosity and without criticism.

Your child is going to ask you thousands of questions through the growing-up years. Some of them will seem trivial; some will be a nuisance. Others will be profound. All of your child's questions are important, however. The way you respond to them will have a great impact on your child's curiosity and ability to think independently. Your child will more likely remember *how* you answer than what you say.

Answer your child's questions . . .

. . . without criticizing your child for asking. Every question deserves an acknowledgment, even if the response is "Let's discuss that later" or "I would rather not answer that question right now." Never make your child feel stupid or ashamed of a question. All questions are worthwhile, even if all questions aren't appropriate or necessary.

. . . with patience. If your child seems to ask you questions just to annoy you, insist that he ask his questions at a later time when you can give him your full attention. Otherwise, take the time to answer fully and ask your child if he understands or has further questions.

. . . as fully as your child needs an answer. We all know the story of the child who asked her father to tell her where her baby sister came from. The father thought the discussion was about sex. The child was looking for the name of the hospital. If your child wants information that you believe would be a burden for his or her level of emotional maturity, tell your child that you will answer the question fully when you believe the time is right.

One young mother was faced with questions from her son about her divorce from his father. She did not feel prepared to answer them yet, so she gave him this analogy. "When you fly to your grandparents' house, I don't ask you to carry your big suitcase. It's too heavy for you. Your carry-on bag is just the right size and weight for you to carry. The answers you want me to give you right now are ones that I think are too heavy for you to carry in your heart. When you are older, you will be better able to carry them."

He understood her reasoning and accepted her refusal to give him the details he wanted. When the time came several years later to know more about his father and the reasons for the divorce, he indeed was much better equipped emotionally to handle the information he received. He said to his mother, "I don't think you should tell my little sister yet. She's still too young to carry this suitcase."

7. *Teach your child that believing and knowing are different and that both are valid in life.* We can believe certain things without knowing them experientially. Not all of human knowledge is subject to verification by the senses. We can learn from others vicariously. The key to acquiring wisdom is our *believing*

attitude toward God and His mysteries, not our *capacity for experience.*

I wish Kendall had known the difference. He was one of the top students in my high school class. His father was a research scientist as well as an engineer who had an excellent reputation in the oil and gas industry. His mother had taught him that everything is subject to testing. She was an agnostic and trained her son to be one, too. Everything in their home was subject to reasoning. If something couldn't be manipulated, it couldn't be tested. If it couldn't be experienced, then it couldn't be evaluated.

Kendall studied at a major university and in the course of experiencing life came to this conclusion, "I can't criticize the value or use of hallucinogenic drugs unless I have experienced them." He overdosed in the process of testing his own theories. After several days in a coma, he awoke to a new life with considerable brain damage.

Teach your child the difference between belief and knowledge. A child can understand that you *know* a certain town is eighteen miles away but you *believe* heaven exists. Teach the value of believing behaviors are right or wrong on the basis of others' experiences and making decisions based on intuition and conscience. Make no apologies for your beliefs, but differentiate them from verifiable facts.

8. Model tolerance for others when they are wrong. Quickly forgive—your child is watching. Don't turn every spoken error into a public debate.

9. Ask questions. If you don't know something, ask someone who does know. Ask questions in a genuine manner—not to bait or taunt a person. Ask in order to learn, and listen intently to the answers. As you model sincere questioning behavior, your child will copy it and be more prone to ask questions in school. And your child will see there's nothing wrong with not knowing—only something wrong with not finding out the answer.

Getting the Best Answers

The most productive and useful answers come as we ask questions that are ...

... focused. Specific and succinct questions are much better than vague ones. "Where is the nearest rest room?" is a much better question than "Would you happen to know if there are rest room facilities available in this building?"

... related to immediate concerns. Questions related to hypothetical situations are rarely productive. "When is lunch?" is a much better question than "What do you suppose is the likelihood that a meal is going to be served midday?"

... aimed at benefit. Questions that have the potential for yielding helpful answers are much better than ones that yield only discussion. "Do you have an air pump?" is much more productive than "Why is there air?"

The High-Powered Question of "Why?"

Perhaps the most potent question in life is "Why?" This question is at the core of the big issues of life: Why am I here? Why did God create me? Why do I feel the way I feel? Why do I act the way I do? Why have faith?

The why question seeks out motivation and intention and therefore fits under the category of values and beliefs. It has to do with the nature of God, humanity, the world, and life in general. Because of this, why questions rarely can be given full answers in a classroom setting. They are best answered in the home.

There are several why questions you need to discuss with your child before the topics come up at school.

"Why should a person not use drugs, alcohol, or prescriptive medicines to excess?" Your child needs to come to school armed with an answer *before* he or she encounters someone selling drugs. Talk to your child about drugs as early as first grade. If you are using chemicals yourself, keep in mind that what you say will always be measured against what you do. Behavior is always a much more powerful lesson than speeches.

"Why should a person wait until marriage before engaging in sexual intercourse?" Your child needs to come to school with the answer *before* he has sex education classes. Sex education classes in the public school system emphasize biological and physiological facts, various sexual orientations, and how to engage in "safe sex." The underlying premise is that young people will engage in sex prior to marriage and that all sexual behaviors are equally acceptable. If you believe otherwise and want your child to act otherwise, you need to build this foundation in the home long before your child hears about sex at school. Start in the early elementary years to talk to your child about values related to sexual behavior.

"Why should a person stay out of gangs?" A child needs to have reasons that will hold up to peer pressure. Generally speaking, the child who has a strong and supportive family is less susceptible to peer influence than a child who has absentee parents or weak family ties. Most children gravitate toward gangs in order to find acceptance and love. Rather than criticizing certain individuals, speak positively about your child, his future and potential, and the love you have for him.

"Why should a person pursue an education?" Your child needs to hear the value you place on learning. If your child knows that learning is important to you, it will be more important to him or her, especially as he watches you engage in research, ask questions, and even take courses in order to keep learning.

"Why should a person seek peace?" Children see a world that is marked by violence. They see violence on television and movie screens and read about it in newspapers. The result is that many children regard their own neighborhoods as far more dangerous than they actually are. Children today are much more fearful than they were a generation ago. A child needs to come to school armed with a mind-set toward pursuing peace rather than violence.

Research Questions: Who and Where?

A child will instinctively ask the question, "Why?" Two of the most potent questions you can teach your child to ask are these:

- Who knows the answer?
- Where can I find the answer?

These two questions are at the core of basic research, and they are vital to a child's education.

The best way to teach research behavior is to model it, by conducting your own research openly before your children. When you don't have an answer, whom do you call on the phone? Whom do you ask? Explain why you choose certain resources over others. Consult reference books often—an atlas, a dictionary, a volume of an encyclopedia—and make the material familiar to your child.

When I was a child, I often asked my mother how to spell certain words or what certain words meant. I can still hear her say, "Look it up." After a while, I quit asking and headed straight for the dictionary. Today, children tend to head for the spell-check feature on their home computers!

Most children would rather learn something new than be entertained passively. Active learning and playing are much more fun to children, although the TV-addicted child may need time adjusting to the effort required. Given the option of trying out a new game or watching a video, children nearly always choose the activity.

A child rarely asks questions of a television set. Give your child something to think about. Put a book in her hands and turn off the tube. Introduce her to the wonderful worlds contained in encyclopedias and art books.

Also introduce your child to experts and friends of yours who have had unusual experiences. Let her ask questions, such as "What is the most interesting place you have visited?" and "What was the most unusual experience you had in that place?"

Information is taught, but a spirit of learning is more readily *caught*. Children who are around people who are interested in learning tend to be more curious about life.

Who and where questions relate to learning skills. A child who comes to school eager to know "Who said that?" or "Who can give that answer?" or "Where can I learn that?" is well on his way to becoming a good student.

The Priority Question: When?

The question of "When?" is not only a matter of telling time. It is the chief question in the study of history, and it is also critical to the development of these learning skills: setting priorities, establishing sequence, and following instructions.

Help your child see that certain information is prerequisite to other information. A child must understand that a whole can be divided into parts before he will ever be able to understand fractions. He or she needs to see that certain tasks are best done in a specific order. These lessons can be taught quite easily in the flow of everyday life. For example, if you are cutting a pie, cut it into six pieces and ask your child to count the number of people present. Then, as you serve the pie, point out that "Uncle Mac gets one sixth of the pie, Aunt Louise gets one sixth, Cousin Bobby gets a sixth" and so forth. As you help your child pick up his room, point out the advantage of dusting off the furniture before vacuuming and the advantage of vacuuming a hard surface before mopping it.

If your child asks you when something is likely to happen, be as accurate as possible. At the earliest possible age, give your child a watch and a calendar and show her how to use them. These two tools are vital to our culture.

Teach your child how to tell time on both analog and digital clocks. (I recently met a first grader who was mystified by an analog clock. He had no idea it was a clock! Every clock he had ever seen had been a digital one.) Show your child how to make a schedule, and when he is assigned his first term paper, help him map out incremental steps toward completing the project.

Practical Questions: What and How?

The two giant questions related to the schooling process are "What?" and "How?" Most concepts are explained to children in terms of what and how questions: What is this? What does this mean? How does this work? How are these two similar, or different?

There are five very practical what and how questions you need to teach at home.

1. What is the best way to get from here to there? This is the question of map reading. As you travel, keep maps in your vehicle, and let your child help you navigate. Even if you are running errands around town, let your child help you decide which route to take and to back up his reasons with evidence or argument.

This is also the question of goal setting. Help a child learn to set goals, break those goals down into smaller tasks, and then develop a plan for accomplishing them. You may want to encourage your child by plotting progress on a chart or graph.

When my brother was in Little League, he had a goal of striking out a hundred batters. He knew that he had four years to reach that goal. His annual goal, therefore, was to strike out twenty-five batters a season. The schedule generally included at least a dozen games, each with seven innings. He knew he would probably get to pitch in at least half of the games for at least a few innings, so he carefully calculated that he had to strike out at least four batters a game. All in all, it was a realistic goal and one he achieved the middle of his third year. He had a large chart taped to the inside of a cupboard in his room, and on that chart he carefully kept track of those he struck out as well as his hits and home runs. He had a plan for getting from point A to point B, and today in his business he still is an expert in mapping out a sales strategy and quotas.

The skills of following directions and making plans are critical to school success.

2. How does this work? This is the question that is crucial to the safe operation of all machinery and tools. Show your child how things work and how to use them safely and efficiently. Guide her first efforts and monitor her practice. Set guidelines for when certain pieces of equipment can be used, and stick by those guidelines.

In a broader sense, talk to your child about the way various systems work, such as the different branches of government. When you visit an airport or train station, talk about the different jobs and how they're interrelated. Talk about the systems that are necessary so that planes operate on schedule and luggage arrives at the same time as passengers. Talk about what controls need to be in place to keep two trains off the same track or to keep two planes from colliding in midair. Give your child a sense that the world is at work—that various mechanisms are continually in operation.

Children also can see that relationships tend to work along certain lines. There are unspoken relational and societal laws, such as manners and courtesy, that are part of the way things work in our culture. So are acts of kindness.

Nature also has a way of working. Talk about how things grow. Talk about how the air, water, and land interrelate and must be kept pure and in balance. Talk about the systems of a child's body and how the brain works better when it is adequately fed and the body has had enough sleep.

The school system works in certain ways. Talk to your child about why certain things are done at school and the value of grades, grade levels, teachers, and so forth.

As your child learns more about how certain things work, you will be in a better position to teach your child answers to the next question.

3. How can I fix what is broken? This question has two built-in implications: Many things are worth fixing, and most things can be fixed. Don't be too quick to fix what your child has broken, especially if he broke it carefully or willfully. Let your child work to replace the item. He will value the replacement more and likely handle it with greater care. Granted, if the item is very expensive, your child may not be able to pay for it in full; still, he should be required to pay part. Help your child fix items that are fixable—a bicycle chain, a flat tire, a ripped hem or seam.

Breaches in relationships are often "fixed" through sincere repentance and asking for forgiveness. To restore a broken relationship, some change in behavior is generally required. Teach your child that behavior is subject to the will. Even a young child is capable of changing her behavior and attitude.

I once heard a mother tell her six-year-old daughter, who

was crying loudly and generally making a scene in a crowded restaurant, "You have two choices. You either can continue to cry, and we will go home where you can have a peanut butter sandwich and then go directly to bed, or you can stop crying and choose to have a good time and a good meal in this restaurant, which, I remind you, is the place where you wanted to eat tonight."

The child sputtered, "I don't want to decide."

"Then I will assume that you want to go home because you are still crying, and you obviously don't want to stay."

The child stopped crying but continued to pout. The mother insisted, "That isn't enough. You must also choose to have a good time."

The child thought for a few seconds and then said, "I want to stay." Her attitude changed dramatically in a matter of minutes.

That lesson is invaluable for parents. Children do have control over their emotions, and they can make choices regarding both their behavior and their attitudes, unless they are physically or mentally ill.

How does fixing attitudes relate to school?

Children often don't "feel" like going to school. They may say they don't like school. Generally what they don't like is making the effort to go. If there's a genuine problem with a relationship or a subject matter, other behaviors will crop up—nightmares, bed-wetting, angry outbursts.

The child who doesn't want to go to school on a given day is best advised, "You need to make a better choice. Choose to be happy at school today. Choose to get along with your teacher and classmates. Choose to learn all you can." A child can fix his attitude about school. He can change his behavior if it is bad.

Every child has days in which he or she doesn't perform his best. A bad quiz score or an embarrassment in reading group can be generalized to an attitude of "I'm no good at this." A child needs to be reassured that she can "fix" poor school performance. The remedy might be extra studying or tutoring. Never let your child conclude that she is incapable of learning a particular subject.

A number of years ago I set aside one hour of a semester's course for conducting a study of various testing methods. The test materials required a student to score his own paper and come up with a breakdown of answers by percentage. I let my students know the exercise had nothing to do with their grade for the course, and I promised to let them know the results of the experiment during the next class session. Most of them dove eagerly into the materials. One of the students, however, came to my desk shortly after the exercise began and said, "I can't do this."

"What part don't you understand, Sarah?" I asked.

"I understand the exercise but I can't finish it because I don't know how to do the scoring at the end."

"Which part of the scoring don't you understand?" I asked.

Big tears welled up in Sarah's eyes. "I don't know how to do percentages."

"Oh," I said. "I'll figure that for you if you want. And, if you want to come by my office some time, I'll teach you how to figure percentages. It probably won't take more than five or ten minutes."

Sarah became visibly nervous at that point and said, "I've never been able to figure percentages. I'm just not good at math and never have been."

"You were probably taught poorly," I said, refusing to give up.

"I had lots of teachers and even a tutor," she said firmly. "I'm not good at math, and I don't see any reason to try after so many years. It only upsets me. I can't do math... and neither can my mother."

That was that. Sarah left the room, and we never did have a chance to talk further about percentages. We did, however, talk a little more about Mom and math. Just as I suspected, her mother had convinced her that some people just aren't capable of doing math. Sarah's mother couldn't work math problems, and she didn't expect her daughter to work them.

In contrast was Karl, a student in an informal tutorial session I conducted for foreign students. Karl was from Germany and had a difficult time pronouncing the consonant V. It nearly always came out as a W unless he was very deliberate in his pronunciation. Karl had a sense of humor about this. Every time he said a V word, he made a major point of attempting to pronounce it correctly and slowly. Within a few weeks, however, Karl no longer needed to exaggerate his pronunciation. He had mastered the ability to pronounce his V's.

At one point I said to Karl, "I admire you and all of the foreign students for coming to the United States and attempting to study in a foreign language. I can't imagine taking on college level courses in German."

He said, "My parents both speak five languages. They believe no language is impossible and that a person can learn to speak any language so that he sounds like a native speaker."

"What do you think?" I asked.

"I think the same thing. It may take extra effort, but it's possible."

What a difference between Karl and Sarah in their attitudes toward subject matter.

A child may not be able to fix something perfectly, but he nearly always can improve it to some degree.

4. How will I pay for this? This is the question underlying budgets. It is also the question that helps us evaluate the amount of effort we have to exert to achieve the things we want in life.

We pay for things in various ways: with money, in time, and in effort. Everything we have or achieve costs something.

In a very concrete way, you can help your child learn this lesson by teaching her how to spend her allowance or earnings wisely. You can open up a savings account for your child and help her save a little of everything she earns. You can teach how to weigh value against price and make informed purchasing decisions—whether buying a can of peas in the grocery store or a new skateboard.

I have known a number of college students who didn't have a clue what their education was costing their family financially. Mom and Dad had always paid for everything in life, and now Mom and Dad were paying for room, board, tuition, books, fees, clothes, gasoline, laundry, and entertainment. I asked one young man whose parents were providing him everything, "What do *you* do?"

He said, "I'm supposed to study and get good grades."

A year after this young man graduated from college, he and I had an opportunity to talk again. "How's the *real* world?" I asked.

"It's tough," he said. "Do you know how much things cost these days?"

For a student to appreciate the value of an education, he needs to work for at least part of it. It may be the clothes-and-pizza part of the budget or the amount required for books and lab fees. Handing a child everything on a platter until college is over does little to prepare him for the challenges of paying bills and living on a budget.

5. *"What more is there to know?"* There's always more to know, more to learn, more to experience. Don't let your child sell his own learning ability short or shortchange himself when it comes to studying.

One young man told me toward the end of the semester that he was a premed major. Frankly, I was surprised. Sam made low C's and rarely studied. His assignments obviously were completed the hour before class, and his quiz and exam scores revealed that he had read very little of the course textbook.

"That's a tough major, Sam," I commented.

"Being a doctor is all I've ever wanted to be," he said.

"Do you like science?" I asked.

"Pretty much."

That wasn't the answer I had heard from other premed majors I had known throughout the years. I probed further. "What do you think you're going to like best about being a doctor?" I asked him.

"The money," Sam replied.

This young man evidently understood little of what it takes to get into medical school, to get through medical school, and to get into a residency or ultimately to set up a practice. He didn't have an inkling how much debt he was likely to accrue before he had a position in which he earned what most people would consider a very average salary. He obviously didn't understand the basic economics of medicine in today's world and the high cost of malpractice insurance, modern technology, and general overhead.

More important, Sam did not appear to realize how important it was for him not to take lightly any of the information related to medicine he needed to know. The questions he missed on his medical school exams just might involve the information needed to save a life! If Sam approached his other studies the same way he had approached Oral Communication 101, he was going to be a student who always just skimped by and graduated in the bottom half of his class. I certainly wouldn't want him to be my physician.

Don't let your child skate by in school. Encourage her to put in extra effort, even if it isn't required.

This may sound contradictory to our earlier discussion about school performance versus an attitude of learning. It isn't. A good student's attitude is this: Learn all you can. Don't settle for a smattering of information or a half-baked understanding. Seek to become an expert in one area and an informed generalist in the rest. Not for a grade. Not to impress. But simply because knowing more about a topic is better than knowing less!

If school tasks are easy for your child, take on the responsibility of challenging your child with more difficult material.

I distinctly remember the day my mother announced to me that I could no longer check out books from the "little kids" room at the local library. I suspect now that she was tired of lugging home a dozen small books twice a week, only to watch me whip through them and ask when we were going back to the library. At her insistence, I entered the room containing thick books with very few pictures. I checked out my first novel that day: *The Secret Garden.* It wasn't my last.

Was Mom pushing me? Not really. She was opening a door of greater opportunity. She was helping me discover a much broader and ultimately more interesting world. I got no credit for reading library books. I impressed nobody by the number of books I read or the subjects I explored. What I did get was a good education and a growing thirst to learn more.

Enhancing the Willingness to Ask

In order to research answers to life's questions, your child needs basic tools.

A library card. Make sure your child has a library card and goes to the library often. Challenge him to explore new areas—including fiction, nonfiction, biography, and history.

Monitor the books he selects before you check them out. (I recently went to the library with a godchild and was dismayed at the number of books we opened that dealt with occultic themes or "dark" subjects. Keep in mind, too, that a good many novels today are very graphic in their depictions of violent and sexual acts.)

A good student once said to me, albeit with a groan, "My parents always thought my having a library card was far more important than my having a credit card or a driver's license." He may have felt deprived; he actually was far richer than most of his peers.

A growing library of his own. Buy books for your child. Insist that your child treat books with care. Put a bookplate in the front of his books so your child will associate his name with them and value them more.

Invest in the classics—the tales that have stood the test of time. These are books worth rereading. Include a couple of books of poetry, too, or a children's volume of Shakespeare.

Reference materials. Make adequate reference books available to your child, within your home if possible. Make certain your child has access to a good dictionary appropriate to his reading level, as well as a good atlas, a book of famous quotations, a thesaurus, and a basic encyclopedia (in one volume or more). If purchasing these books isn't feasible, make certain your child can get to the library frequently to consult them.

In providing these tools, you are giving your child a major boost in asking and then answering the questions of life.

Chapter 6

SIMPLE TRUTH

Lesson #3: You Are What You Take In

We've all heard the phrase, "You are what you eat."

What we take into our lives—willfully or subconsciously—defines us to a great extent. Our intake is not only material substance; it's also feelings drawn from relationships and intuitions drawn from experience.

How do we decide what our intake will be? First, let's differentiate between what we want and need.

A person needs very few things. The psychologist Abraham Maslow identified a hierarchy of human needs. At the base are the material needs of food, water, and air. A human can live for weeks without food, for days without water, but only for minutes without air. Higher up the hierarchy is shelter. At the top are love and a sense of purpose in life. Maslow's premise is that a person must have his most basic needs met before he can address higher level needs. For example, a drowning person needs air more than social acceptance.

Vital though they are, all of these needs differ from wants. Life and health relate to needs; whereas *quality* of life relates to fulfilling wants.

Three basic criteria govern consumption, whether we're consuming food or ideas:

1. Not all things are beneficial for consumption. Just as

poison can be found in food, water, or air, so poisonous ideas and feelings can exist. Purity is desirable in all that we consume. We benefit when we take in only that which builds us up, energizes us, and give us a sense of meaning and purpose in life.

2. *Excess consumption results in burden.* Too much food and not enough exercise results in fat, which slows a body down and makes it susceptible to disease. Too much conceptual and spiritual overload and a person can find himself suffering from depression, brainwashing, or various forms of delusion and dementia.

3. *The healthy person not only must take in adequate nutrients but also have a way of eliminating waste.* In physical terms, a person must have good digestive and elimination systems. In spiritual terms, a person must have a healthy means of absorption and expression.

A look at needs, wants, and consumption criteria leads us to a major concept: choice.

Much of what a child encounters in school is a prescribed curriculum. Elementary curriculums are virtually set, with the occasional opportunity to participate in a music program or a study hall during a regular school day. Slightly more choice is granted to high school students, but the parameters are still limited, especially if a student is college-bound. College is usually the first place a student has the opportunity to choose what to study and when to study it, and even there, general education classes fill up most of the first two years and a specific set of courses is prescribed for a major and minor. Elective courses rarely amount to more than fifteen percent of a student's total college credit hours in a baccalaureate program.

By comparison, your child faces thousands of out-of-school choices—from part-time job and career options, to the music he hears, to the friends he chooses, to the foods he eats at lunch, to the clothes he wears, to the ways in which he decorates his room, to the things he purchases with his discretionary money.

Some teachers do make it a priority to help students apply curriculum content to life choices. Never assume that a school curriculum will help your child make practical decisions in life.

Give Your Child Basic Life Skills

It is up to you to equip your child with certain life skills that will help him make sound choices for physical, mental, emotional, and spiritual well-being.

These life skills include the twelve listed below, each of which are covered only briefly in a couple of paragraphs. Most of these skill statements include the word *manage*. Management covers both acquisition and application of a resource. Another word for management is *stewardship*.

1. How to manage money. School math classes frequently include word problems that relate to earning or spending, but you are your child's best financial advisor. You're the one who attaches value to working, saving, and giving. You're the best one to show your child how to weigh cost factors against value; to differentiate between needs and wants.

I once asked a class of college students to fill out a fairly extensive questionnaire, indicating the level of skills they felt they had acquired prior to college using the categories of *totally inexperienced, novice, adequate,* and *expert.* Eighty percent of the students labeled themselves as totally inexperienced or novices in these very practical areas of money management: balancing a check book register against a bank statement, investing in stocks and bonds, buying insurance, completing tax forms, making a budget, planning for retirement, getting a loan, calculating interest rates, and starting a business. None of these students were majoring or minoring in business. I have no idea where or when in life they thought they were going to acquire these skills.

Certainly not all parents can be financial experts, but they *can* make sure their high school students have checking accounts. They can talk over investments, insurance, retirement plans, and loan structures with their children as they make decisions in their own lives. Parents can teach their children how to make a budget and live within it.

Debt is a psychological burden to most people. And we are a nation deeply in debt, both individually and corporately. A parent cannot rely on a school curriculum to teach a child how to get out or stay out of debt.

2. How to manage health. Schools teach biology, basic hygiene, and certain health-related subjects, including sex education. They offer athletic programs, and many require physical education classes. This doesn't mean, however, that school will teach your child the basics of nutrition and exercise. That's up to you.

Maintain an active lifestyle for your children. Don't let your child become a couch potato. Insist that he go outside and play and exercise those large muscle groups in his legs and arms. Take vigorous walks with your child. Let your child see you engaging in stretching exercises that enhance flexibility.

Feed your child nutritious foods and provide supplements if necessary. As much as possible, eliminate sugar from your child's diet. Excessive amounts of sugar result in mood swings that directly affect a child's ability to learn.

Never send your child to school without a good breakfast that includes protein. A good breakfast is a glass of juice, a piece of whole-grain toast or a bowl of whole-grain cereal, and protein in the form of milk (perhaps fortified with additional protein powder or a scoop of dried skim milk) or eggs. This is a breakfast that sticks with a child throughout a morning of learning. Pack a school lunch that includes protein and sets up a child to have energy in the middle of the afternoon. Avoid sugary cereals and keep candy bars and sugar-laden fruit drinks out of your child's lunch pail.

Most elementary teachers will tell you that they have no difficulty in determining which children have had a good breakfast by eleven o'clock on any given morning. Those children who have come to school after a protein-rich breakfast are calmer, more focused, more alert, and better able to think logically. They are in a better frame of mind to learn. Those who have come to school without breakfast or after a sugar-filled breakfast tend to be lethargic, restless, and easily distracted.

A classroom teacher can instruct in the mechanics of how to bathe or how to engage in sexual intimacy. Only a parent can teach a child the importance of cleanliness or the appropriateness of certain sexual acts.

Teach your child when and how to rest and relax effectively. Those skills are rarely taught these days, but they're vital in combating stress. Make sure your child gets enough sleep. When he's ill, insist that he do what is necessary to get well, including staying in bed. If a physician prescribes a medication for your child, make sure he takes it and only in the dosage prescribed.

Send your child to school every morning with his face washed, his teeth brushed, his hair clean and combed, and his clothes clean. Insist that he wash his hands before eating and after using the toilet. Tell him when it's appropriate to see a school nurse or ask to be excused from a classroom. Children don't automatically engage in good hygiene. Somebody must teach them the basic skills and insist they be repeated until they're habit. Don't expect a schoolteacher to do this.

Finally, teach your child how to cook. When I was a seventh grader, I had an hour of home economics each week.

We learned how to cook oatmeal, poach an egg, bake a cake (from a mix), and prepare a simple meal selecting foods from the four major food groups. Those were the only cooking lessons I ever had in school. Everything else I know about cooking I have learned through experimentation or through watching my mother and grandmother, both of whom were excellent cooks. It was from Mom that I learned how to make jams and jelly, plant and harvest a garden, and separate honey from honeycomb, and it was from Dad that I learned how to clean fish.

A parent need not be a gourmet cook in order to teach the basics of food preparation. Let your child help you make salads and prepare casseroles. Send your teenager to the store occasionally. Insist that your children help you clean up the kitchen.

3. How to manage shelter. No doubt your child will study everything from tepees to igloos in school. If he is a Scout, he will probably learn to set up a tent or make a basic lean-to at summer camp. He will not learn about rental leases, mortgages, the value of insulation, yard maintenance, or basic plumbing repairs. He may study electricity in science, but he won't learn how to change a lightbulb or fuse.

Let your child help you around the house. When the time comes to repaint or wallpaper your teenager's room, let her do it or help you. When the time comes to shop for new appliances or carpeting, take your child along. Let her see what options there are.

Most parents have said more times than they can count, "Clean up your room." But how many parents have ever really taught their children *how* to clean a room? Does your child know how to pick up clothes and sort them, fold them, hang them up, or store them for easy access? Does he know the best way to dust, vacuum, wash windows, or use a broom?

When I was in college, a girl down the hall from me in

the dormitory had a private room. There were few private rooms available, and I was curious to see how a private room compared to a double occupancy room. Having a room all to oneself seemed like an amazing luxury, and it seemed no accident that this girl came from a wealthy family. One day I took advantage of her open door and peeked in.

I was shocked. Clothes were strewn everywhere. There wasn't one square inch of the floor or bed that wasn't piled with at least twelve inches worth of clothes, shoes, books, or sundries. She laughingly said later that when her closets were empty, that was a clue to sort out her clothes and send them to the laundry.

On the questionnaire mentioned earlier, I asked students how adept they felt they were at certain chores. Ninety-four percent of these college sophomores did not know where to turn off the water to a house, where the circuit breaker box was, or how to retrieve something from the drain of a kitchen sink. Let me assure you, no college teacher was going to tell them.

Unless you are wealthy and are assured that your child will always be wealthy and be able to hire a maid, you're wise to teach your child how to keep a room neat enough to accommodate another person!

4. *How to provide clothing.* Even young children these days are pretty smart shoppers. They recognize brands and know what they like. Very few can tell you how to care for various types of clothing, however. A student once gave a very humorous and informative speech titled, "Mom Never Told Me Not to Wash Rayon." Her speech included a number of props and detailed how to wash items of various fabric content and color. The entire class followed her presentation intently. One student commented as she left class, "I've been doing it all wrong! I learned more today about laundry than I've learned in all my life!"

A school curriculum covers how much flax is exported by a certain nation or which states have the best soil for growing cotton, but no classroom teacher teaches your child how to read a clothing label, do laundry, stitch a button onto a shirt, mend a hem, let out or take in a seam, iron a blouse, remove spots, or choose styles that last more than one season.

Send your child to school every morning in clean clothes, including clean socks and underwear. Teach your child at an early age how to sort his clothes for washing, how to do a load of laundry, and how to iron. Teach your child how to polish a pair of shoes.

5. How to manage people. Everybody is a supervisor at some point in life. Parents certainly are. Managing people means simply choosing, as much as possible, the people in your life and making good relationships. In a social group, the goal is to help everyone have a good time. In a task-oriented group, the goal is stay focused and be as productive as possible. But groups are rarely task-oriented only. There's always a social dimension, too.

A study done by a management group several years ago revealed that most employees in our nation felt their work environment was a more important factor in job satisfaction than salary or benefits. Relationships are what makes any group affiliation meaningful and satisfying, no matter if it's a family, a church, a company, a club, or a school.

What can you do to help your child in this area? As discussed in an earlier chapter, see that your child is a member of many different types of groups. Within those various groups, make sure that your child has an opportunity to be both leader and follower.

At times, let your child be responsible for decisions that involve your entire family. For example, one night a month, you might let the child plan the dinner menu. Or one day of a vacation, let the child choose the family activity.

One of the most effective means of developing relational skills in a child is not with human beings but with pets. A child can benefit greatly from having primary responsibility for a cat or dog—including its grooming and periodic trips to the veterinarian. Pets are a great way to instill a sense of daily responsibility for another living thing and to show a child the advantages of discipline (as the child teaches a pet what to do and not do). If you live in an environment that isn't conducive to keeping a cat or dog, consider a bird or an aquarium of fish. The type of pet isn't as important as the lessons learned in caring for it.

Older children at times should be given limited management responsibility for younger children. They may baby-sit or perhaps work as a teacher's aide in a Sunday school class.

Help your child choose friends wisely. Point out what a good friend is—including the importance of loyalty, keeping confidences, spending time together, having a balance between giving and receiving, and sharing decision-making power. Point out to your child that he or she has the privilege of choosing friends and building a friendship that lasts. In helping your child make friends, you are helping prepare him or her for a good marriage later in life.

Teachers manage classrooms. They rarely give students an opportunity to do so. Your child will learn most of what he knows about managing other people outside the schoolhouse.

6. How to manage nature. We've already mentioned the value of pets. Your child's ability to manage nature also extends to plants. Schools today place great emphasis on environmental studies. Your child is likely to know a great deal about the rain forests of the world and about how factories pollute rivers. It's not uncommon to find that children are far more concerned about recycling than their parents are.

Periodically take a ride through the countryside. Stop to ask questions of farmers about the crops or orchards on their acreage. Give your child a sense of what the growing seasons are all about. Visit the same area once a season for a year. Any farm looks different in winter, spring, summer, and at harvest-time.

If possible, plant at least one fairly large garden with your child. Try a mix of flowers and vegetables. Let the child discover what is involved in preparing the soil, choosing appropriate species, planting, weeding, cultivating, irrigating, dealing with pests and weather or wind damage, and harvesting. If planting a garden isn't possible, give your child experiences that are appropriate for your living space: growing a sweet potato plant or an avocado tree or planting an herb garden in a window box.

Teach your child to read the signs of the weather. Your child will learn in school about various cloud formations and perhaps even how to make a rain gauge. You will be his best teacher, however, when it comes to recognizing the signs of changing seasons. In sum, help your child develop an overall sensitivity to the natural world.

7. *How to travel.* Children travel more today than they have in any previous generation. I rarely take a flight without seeing at least a half dozen children traveling by themselves. There's more to travel than knowing how to get on and off a plane. It includes knowing what to pack and what to leave at home, knowing how to plan a trip, read a map, and get to a destination on time. It's knowing how to behave in a hotel, dine in a restaurant, maintain a car en route, and meet people easily. Travel is making choices about food and shelter and taking precautions on the road.

Nearly every white-collar occupation now involves travel. No classroom teacher lectures on how to avoid jet lag or wash out undies in a hotel sink. You are your child's best travel guide.

Travel with your children as much as possible. Introduce

them to people and places they have only read about. There's no greater educational experience. Not only does it broaden a person's world view, it also gives a person confidence and stimulates curiosity. Perhaps no other venture provides so many opportunities for solving problems and making decisions. Travel helps a child become more independent and culturally aware.

8. How to manage time. Schools run on tight schedules. Bells ring and people move. Apart, perhaps, from factory work, this isn't the way the rest of life is. It certainly isn't the way nonwork hours are structured. There are several excellent ways to teach your child how to manage time.

Have your child keep a schedule. That includes getting up, eating, and going to bed at designated times. Don't vary the schedule except for special occasions.

I recall only one night when I was in elementary school that I was allowed to stay up past ten o'clock. The opportunity was a rare, total lunar eclipse! To prepare for that opportunity, of course, I had to take a lengthy nap. Otherwise, I never would have been able to stay awake long enough to watch the moon be wiped out of the sky ever so mysteriously by the earth's own shadow, only to reappear a few moments later.

I am amazed today at the great number of children who routinely stay up until the wee hours of the morning. Television rating organizations have estimated that up to forty percent of the after ten o'clock evening viewing audience is children under the age of twelve! Teachers see the difference. Scores of children enter any one school system each morning with their eyes half open.

Don't let your child overbook himself. Put a limit on the number of lessons, team commitments, and clubs in your child's life. Make sure she has plenty of playtime with friends as well as time alone studying.

Help your child map out schedules. There are times your

child needs to plan ahead to complete a project. Keep a master calendar in your home for noting your child's major events, games, and performances.

If your child is taking lessons, insist that he practice. Set regular practice times. There's an advantage to sitting at a piano for twenty minutes every day. Children who practice regularly—no matter if it's music, dance, typing, or shooting baskets—not only improve their ability but also develop an inner persistence to complete tasks. They also concentrate better on schoolwork and are more likely to complete a lesson in one sitting.

9. How to manage machinery. Children are fascinated by gadgets from the time they are just a few weeks old! Your child will encounter most of the machines he learns to operate outside the classroom. Just about the only ones he'll use in school will be calculators, typewriters, and computers, as well as an assortment of scales and rulers (and perhaps a Bunsen burner). Even those basic tools aren't available in all schools.

When I was a child, I was responsible for loading the dishwasher after most meals. I did this reluctantly at times and enthusiastically at others. What I learned in the process, however, was how to get the most dishes into the machine and still have them all come out clean. It was an exercise in space management as much as the management of a machine!

There are several important facts to learn about machines.

- Machines have component parts.
- They are nearly always linked to larger systems of some type.
- They may or may not save time and energy.
- They need to be maintained.
- They ultimately wear out or break.
- They nearly always provide an opportunity to be in-

jured. Therefore, they usually have safety precautions associated with them.

Teach your child these lessons about machines as you help her learn to handle the various tools and machines in your own home. By teaching your child how to operate machines safely, you are also giving her an opportunity to exercise problem solving, discernment, and responsibility.

10. How to train children. Schools don't teach parenting, and yet most likely your child be a parent one day. Much of how your child parents will be based on how he was parented—in other words, he'll be copying you.

The bulk of what a parent teaches is actually classified as training. Training is a specialized form of instruction based on physical behaviors, routine, and repetition. The result of training is habit.

It is important for a child to do certain things regularly and frequently. For example, insist that your child wash his hands before *each* meal and brush his teeth after *each* meal he eats at home. Require your child to attend Sunday school and church with you *every* Sunday. Insist that your child save a certain percentage of *every* allowance payment he receives.

It will be up to you to decide what behaviors you want your child to exhibit the rest of his life. In order for those behaviors to become habit, they need to be instilled at a young age.

When my brother and I were in elementary school, my father taught my brother how to open doors and pull out chairs for my mother and me. He doesn't even think twice today before doing it.

I have had a number of students in my classes who wouldn't dream of addressing me without adding a "ma'am" to their sentence. They didn't acquire that habit because somebody told them in a newspaper article that it was a good thing to do. They learned it from their parents or guardians.

It will be up to you to train your child to write thank-you notes, use good table manners, and learn various other social amenities. You'll be the one to train your child in how to introduce people and greet them with a handshake. Don't expect these lessons to be taught at school, even if your child goes to a privileged private school. These are lessons best modeled at home.

The habits of bathing daily, caring for hair and nails, and other personal hygiene habits are all subject to training. In fact, most of the life skills in this chapter are best learned through repetition until the behavior becomes a habit.

In the intellectual arena, you will be wise to teach your child to memorize passages of Scripture or famous edifying quotes at an early age. You may want to learn selected verses together. Then, through the years, renew what you have learned and recite words of comfort to each other. You will be training your child to find ready counsel all his life.

11. How to communicate nonverbally. Teachers specialize in verbal communication—reading, writing, speaking—and to a certain extent expression in art and music. It is up to the parent to teach nonverbal skills—nuances of gesture and facial expression, how close to stand, how loud to talk. Your child learns these skills copying you.

Encourage your child to take lessons in art or music. His or her ability to communicate will broaden as well as coordination and awareness of culture at large.

12. How to maintain a spiritual equilibrium. No teacher or school can teach spiritual lessons as a parent can. In public schools, spiritual subjects are off limits. You will have to be your child's pastor and Sunday school teacher, teaching the application of Scripture, the taking of Communion elements, giving alms, and operating in the realm of spiritual gifts.

Many parents leave this job totally to clergy and church youth workers. However, just as with other lessons, healthful spiritual behaviors are *best* learned at home from parents who model them. Your home is the best place for your child to learn how to read the Bible and sing songs of praise. And it's the best place for your child to wrestle with values and doubts he may have about his faith. No matter what you say, your child ultimately will copy your patterns of church attendance and giving.

Don't be discouraged at the vast amount of content these twelve skills cover. Most of these lessons can be taught in the normal routines of life. The key principle to remember is this: Include your child. If you're going to the bank, take your child along. Let her watch you make transactions. If you're cleaning out the gutters, let your child participate. Take your child to church regularly and pray often with your child. Talk about why you make certain decisions or do things in a certain way. Explain . . . and help . . . and encourage your child's participation.

Don't think of yourself as a teacher so much as a companion along the way. Keep in mind that the disciples who followed Jesus didn't learn from Him in a classroom. They learned by walking and talking with Him on a daily basis and then by doing what He had shown them. And your child will learn from you, day by day.

Defining the Unnecessary

One of my favorite movies is *Short Circuit,* a rather innocent little movie about a robot that comes to life and has an insatiable appetite for input. One of the things the robot learns is that not all input is good. And that's one of the main lessons you need to teach your child.

There are many, many things in life your child doesn't

need to know. He doesn't need to know how to manufacture a bomb. He doesn't need to know hunger or abandonment. He doesn't need to know what it's like to be high on drugs or drunk from alcohol.

You need to express to your child that there are many things he or she doesn't need to experience and therefore will *not* be allowed to experience them in your home. As long as you have responsibility for your child, you have authority over your child and what he does in your home and community.

Part of asking the right questions in life is asking what is harmful or unnecessary. In addition to asking about what is good, your child should ask, "What is bad?" In addition to asking, "What do I need to know?" your child should have a general understanding of what he does not need to know.

There are certain movies and television programs your child doesn't need to see, books and magazines he doesn't need to read, and music he doesn't need to hear. There are certain people he doesn't need to know, places he doesn't need to visit, and experiences he doesn't need to have.

Couch these things in terms of pollution. That is a term most children know today. In a very real way, evil ideas are pollutants of the mind and soul.

Parents need to keep in mind, however, that there are two thrills to which most children gravitate: noise and speed. The entire amusement park and video arcade industry is based on these two factors. Most children love things that go fast, and they respond readily to unusual noises, seemingly the louder the better. Speed and noise are means of escaping reality; they create a fantasy world or signal a break from reality. But too much noise and speed can be harmful.

Insist that your child stay grounded in reality. Don't allow your child to sit in a room filled with blaring music, play video games, or engage in virtual reality videos for great lengths of time. I personally recommend that you limit involvement with video games, including Nintendo, to no more than a half hour a day. The same standard applies to time spent alone listening to music or hooking up to virtual reality. If music is worth hearing for longer than a half hour, it should be music the entire family can enjoy.

Make no apology for denying certain things to your child. Assure him that you are attempting to be the best parent you know how to be and that your goal is not to deprive him but to prepare him for a happy and successful future. Many children ask for things they actually do not want to receive. On more than one occasion, I've heard children say to their parents that they are glad a parent didn't allow them to attend a particular party or go to a particular event. If you have trained your child to appreciate what is good, pure, and excellent, your child will be grateful for your helping him withstand what is evil.

Teach Your Child What Is Harmful

In some cases, you need to be very deliberate in telling your child what is harmful. If you don't have a definition of evil, you need to come up with one. Jesus offered one in John 10:10, when He described the enemy of our souls as a thief who comes to steal, kill, and destroy. Even a young child is able to understand evil when it is defined that way.

Drug abuse robs a person of money and eventually kills a person's ability to make sound judgments and may kill the body. Drug abuse destroys relationships, reputation, and future opportunities for successful employment. Illicit drugs are evil.

Occultic practices are evil. They steal a person's ability to differentiate between right and wrong, kill a person's conscience, destroy life and sensitivity, and may very well destroy a person's ability to experience eternity.

Immorality steals a person's innocence or virginity. Sexually transmitted diseases can kill physically as immorality can destroy the reputation.

Don't just tell your child that certain things are wrong. Give your child a working definition of evil against which to evaluate behavior. When your child asks why you disapprove of certain behaviors, have a reason. If your child is old enough to ask why something is wrong, he's old enough to think through an answer. And he's old enough to understand when you say, "I don't have a lot of reasons that are going to make sense to you right now, but you are going to have to trust me on this. I don't believe this is in your best interest, and as your parent, I have to go with those parental hunches." A child knows when a parent is basing his answers on love—but it never hurts to tell the child one more time, "I say so because I love you."

Ask for the Good

Finally, encourage your child to memorize the following passage of Scripture:

> Whatever things are true, whatever things are noble, whatever things are just, whatever things are pure, whatever things are lovely, whatever things are of good report, if there is any virtue and if there is anything praiseworthy—meditate on these things (Phil. 4:8).

The most potent question your child can ask is, "How do I find the things that are true, noble, just, pure, lovely, and of good report in life?" The answer will lead your child straight to the heart of God and the nature of His Son, Jesus Christ.

Chapter 7

SIMPLE TRUTH

Lesson #4: You Grow Through Giving

Chapter 5 discussed the importance of asking the right questions to get the right input. In this chapter we discuss the right output. Giving is the most noble form of output.

Physical exercise builds strength and adds to flexibility. By the same token, information supplies fodder for the brain. Intellectual and spiritual exercise adds inner strength and a greater ability to relate to others. A person grows in character and wisdom if there is a balance between good mental and spiritual nutrients and related exercise.

Mental and spiritual exercise, however, is not a matter of thinking or feeling. An individual doesn't become strong in the inner person by contemplation. Real strength and ability to grow as a person come from talking and doing. The final application of what is taken into the mind and heart is in the doing—the manner in which life is lived.

In the physical realm, a person benefits most from warm-up stretching followed by aerobic exercise. These are the exercises that keep the muscles supple and strong. In the intellectual and spiritual realm, a child grows through *generous and unselfish giving*.

Rudy was a student who showed me this process in dramatic terms.

When Rudy entered college he was a taker, not a giver. Everything Rudy did was a calculation—he befriended people in very marginal ways in order to extract very high paybacks. He was constantly looking for bargains, shortcuts, and freebies. He bought nothing that wasn't deeply discounted, and he had a very entrenched habit of asking people if he could borrow things that he never seemed to return. Rudy was a user of people and a lover of things.

For a while, Rudy's roommate Tom allowed Rudy to use him. Tom helped Rudy study, allowed him to look over his tests from past courses, and gave to Rudy generous amounts of time, not to mention shampoo, peanut butter, and gasoline. Finally, Tom said, "No more." He confronted Rudy, and as might be expected, Rudy was deeply hurt. He denied all forms of selfish behavior and claimed Tom was the one who was manipulative and self-absorbed.

Tom and I had the opportunity to talk while he was still reeling from his blowup with Rudy. After Tom had let off considerable steam, I asked him, "What is Rudy's background?"

"He didn't grow up poor, if that's what you're getting at," Tom said. "Rudy's parents are quite well off."

"The amount of money you earn or accumulate doesn't have anything to do with either generosity or greed," I said.

"I think greed might be a good word to apply to this situation," Tom said. "Rudy's father is a real wheeler-dealer in the automobile business. He's always looking for a deal, and even though he claims to give deals to others, he's the big winner in nearly all cases."

"Do you have any idea about how Rudy's father treated Rudy when he was growing up?" I asked.

"Not really," Tom replied. "What I do know is that there were five boys in the family, and Rudy is next to youngest. He has talked a lot about how competitive they all were—even down to seeing who could get the biggest helpings of mashed potatoes at dinner. I also know that Rudy rarely calls up to ask his mother and father for anything. I think they're expecting Rudy to figure things out on his own and to make his own way as much as possible."

"Does Rudy have a job?" I asked.

"He just started one," Tom said.

I suggested Tom ride out the next few weeks and see if working at a regular job had any effect on Rudy.

I had Rudy in one of my classes. He was very much a schemer. He was a master of pulling together so-called study groups. I have little doubt that Rudy brought very little to those groups. From what I could tell, he was using them as a shortcut to reading the text. I overheard him a number of times asking other students where they got certain things and how much they had paid for them. He was very bold in asking me to excuse him from attending a required class session so he could attend an automobile auction. "I have to get a car, you know," he said. He pouted for two weeks when I told him that car shopping wasn't a legitimate excuse.

Two years went by before I saw Rudy again. He was a senior. I almost didn't recognize him, not because his appearance had changed so much but because he was doing something I had never expected to see Rudy do. He was helping a student in a wheelchair negotiate a particularly high curb. When he spotted me, he called out and waved.

"That was a nice thing you did," I said as he ran over to walk with me toward the classroom building.

"I've got to make a note of that curb and let the people know that we need a ramp someplace along that side of the street."

"Are you working for an advocacy group?"

"Not really," he said. "I've been volunteering for about a year now at a rehab center.

"How did you get involved in that?" I asked.

"A friend of mine from work was in an accident, and I went to visit him there. He actually dared me to get involved as a volunteer. It's the best thing I've ever done."

"Oh?" I replied.

"Yeah," Rudy continued. "I used to be a real selfish dude. You remember Tom, my first roommate?"

"Yes."

"He tried to tell me that, but I blew him off. I didn't realize until I started working at the rehab center how good I had it and how selfish I really had been. I'm thinking that I might go into physical therapy."

"Really?" I asked. I was still stunned at this great change.

"Yeah. My folks aren't too wild about it. They think I'm wasting my time volunteering at the center and that I should work instead. They also think that if I'm going to be involved in some medical field, I ought to go ahead and be a surgeon so I could make big bucks."

"What do you think?" I asked.

"Frankly, I never helped anybody do anything before I helped John get back on his feet after his car accident. It was a good feeling. I think I'm going to stick to my plan," he said.

Rudy hadn't grown an inch in stature, but he had grown miles taller in his inner person. The difference had taken place as he had given to a fellow human being freely and without an expected return.

Schools and Giving

Schools use the word "give" quite frequently. Teachers give assignments, tests, and grades, and students give reports and answers. In reality, of course, these aren't gifts.

Schools emphasize cooperation and competition. One

puts students together, the other pits students against each other. Neither is an expression of true giving.

Schools require that students share—resources, supplies, space. Sharing is not giving.

In short, schools are not environments in which students are called upon to give to each other, with the exception of valentines once a year. In fact, teachers often admonish students not to give to each other: "Do the assignment on your own" or "Don't copy someone else's work."

The place where giving occurs most, and can be taught best, is the home.

Hallmarks of Quality Giving

Quality giving is marked by three traits.

1. Generosity. The best gifts are those that go beyond minimum expectations. This doesn't mean gifts need to be extravagant. They just need to be better than expected. I'm not implying that a person should go into debt or give to impress others. But we all love generous gifts, those costly in terms of time, effort, or ability. Any gift of time that is precious, of resources that are meager, or talent that might be directed in other ways—and any gift that involves creative expression—is a generous gift.

Generous gifts are often spontaneous, unlinked to a particular holiday or celebration. They depict love that isn't duty-bound.

2. Cheerfulness. The best giving is that done with joy. As the Bible teaches, "So let each one give as he purposes in his heart, not grudgingly or of necessity; for God loves a cheerful giver" (2 Cor. 9:7). If you get what you ask for or give what someone asks of you, it isn't a true gift. A person must have total freedom to make a gift and to do so cheerfully.

3. Anonymity. The best giving is done in secret. If the

recipient must know who gave the gift, one mustn't reveal his identity in a way that makes the person feel uncomfortable or obligated.

Ten Ways to Model Lessons in Giving

How can you teach your child to give generously, cheerfully, and anonymously? Here are ten ways.

1. Teach your child that everything he has in life is a gift from God. Children from the earliest ages can learn that their food, toys, parents, friends, and even the love in their hearts are gifts from their heavenly Father. Ultimately, none of us has total control over any aspect of life. Teach your child to hold on to things gently and appreciate all he is given.

2. Model giving behavior directly to your child. Give an unexpected gift or a surprise party in honor of your child. Treat your child occasionally to something he likes (and which is good for him). Praise him generously and remind him frequently how much you value and love him. Take joy in giving to your child.

I once had a student tell me, "I watched my parents for years as they gave to others. They were very generous in what they gave and in what they said to encourage other people. My mother frequently complimented my friends, including compliments she made about them when their parents were present. They always beamed when she told them how proud she was of their behavior or their school achievements. My father was often asked to give eulogies or present awards because he was such a good speaker. I felt left out. They rarely had a good word to say *to* me *about* me."

Some parents assume their children know how they feel and therefore don't tell them. Your child doesn't know that you love him unless you say so. Don't let your love be a mystery; your child needs to hear that you are proud of him.

Be specific telling your child the things you appreciate about his character. A child needs to know that you see him as an honest, giving, loving, kindhearted, hardworking person. Include all adjectives that may be appropriate! Such encouragement will reinforce these character traits in your child.

A child who is told nothing about himself grows up with giant question marks. A young woman named Yvonne once said to me at a dinner party in my home, "I don't have a clue what my parents think of me."

"Oh, surely you know that they think you're wonderful," I said. Yvonne was beautiful inside and out. She was an excellent student and very talented piano player, and other students frequently referred to her as sweet and generous. She was greatly admired by her peers.

"No," Yvonne replied. "I really don't have a clue. They have told me they love me, but they have never complimented me on my appearance or told me anything they think is good about my character."

Yvonne's comments led me to question several other of my outstanding students about whether their parents had ever made a point of telling them what they liked about them. I was surprised that the majority said, "No."

Eventually I decided to give my students a brief questionnaire. I listed a number of statements, from "I love you" to "I think you have a great smile" to "I'm proud that you are an honest person." I also included some negative statements, such as "I think you're worthless" and "I think you lie more than you tell the truth." I asked them to put a check by the statements they had heard, and I also asked them to identify themselves only by the grade point average they had earned the previous semester in school.

The students with the highest levels of achievement often had heard the statement, "I love you." The students who had low achievement indicated that they had heard a great many negative comments about their character and potential. By and large, however, *neither* group of students had heard very many positive statements about their character from their parents.

In an informal debriefing session, I asked the students if there was anyone other than parents who had applauded their positive character attributes and behavior. The students most frequently cited aunts, uncles, godparents, grandparents, coaches, and club sponsors (especially Scout leaders). One young woman said, "My friends are the only people who have ever told me that I am a good person or that they think I have a bright future."

If you don't give your child a positive evaluation of his character and potential, someone else will. And the person may not be someone who has your child's best interests at heart or has your values and religious beliefs.

I have a personal friend who a number of years ago was involved with a cult for a fairly brief period. What attracted him to that cult was the positive acceptance he received from its members. The cult leaders had told him what his parents never had—that he was an outstanding human being with great potential.

Tell your child in simple, direct terms that you believe in his future, that you see wonderful character traits in him, and that you are proud of who he is as a person.

3. Take your child along with you as you volunteer your time. Let your child see giving in action. As he gets older, he can be encouraged to do volunteer work on his own.

4. Teach your child the difference between gifts from the heart and gifts he asks for. Assure your child that you will provide what he needs in life. Also assure him you delight in giving gifts. But let your child know that you are not obligated to give him everything he asks for.

Limit your child's wish list at Christmas and birthdays.

The child who has a list of twenty things he desires and receives them all is not a child who experiences surprise in opening presents. Some of the joy has been eliminated because the gifts have not come spontaneously from the giver's heart.

5. Let your child overhear you request things from God. Ultimately, we are to make our requests known to God. He is the true supplier of all our needs and the rewarder of those who diligently seek Him (see Phil. 4:6; Heb. 11:6). Turn your child's dependence toward God. Let your child know by your own example that God is who meets our needs, not a person, group, or institution. Our total reliance should be on Him.

Philippians 4:6 says that we are to make our requests known to God in a very specific way:

Without worry. We are not to be anxious as to whether God will meet our needs. He has promised that He will supply what we need. We are to trust Him to do that. A person who asks and receives without worry is a person who is much less likely to hoard or to become greedy.

With thanksgiving. We are to be grateful for both what we have been given and what we will receive. A person who is truly thankful for all that God gives is a person who tends to be much more generous toward others.

Encourage your child's thankfulness and trust by teaching prayers like, "Thank You for hearing my prayer and answering my needs. I'm trusting You, heavenly Father, to give me only those things that You know are for my good. Thank You for always taking care of me and for meeting all of my needs today and in the past."

6. Give your child opportunities to be generous. Periodically suggest that your child go through his toys and pick out some to give away. Let him make the choices. And then ask to whom the items should be given. You should have a few possible donation sites in mind—such as the Salvation Army or a missionary project.

When you're going to visit a sick person, suggest that your child go out into your flower garden and cut a few flowers to take along.

Let her do the choosing and the cutting and also the carrying and giving.

Don't choose gifts for your child to give at birthday parties or Christmas. Sit down with your child and talk about the person who is going to receive the gift. Ask, "What do you think this person would appreciate receiving?" Also talk about how much to spend. Your child should have a part in making the purchase, even if it's only a small percentage of the total cost of the item. Talk about where the best place is to shop. Also talk about appropriate gifts that your child might make. Let your child help wrap the present and write any accompanying gift card. Let your child have an active say in what is given and how.

From time to time, say to your child, "Let's do something nice for ____" and name the person of your choice. Or you might say, "Let's do something nice for somebody this Saturday. Who should it be?"

The person might be someone your child knows well or perhaps has never even met. It may be a person who has material needs or a person who has no financial or material problems. Let your child see you giving gifts to people regardless of their wealth. People of all socioeconomic levels need gifts that express love. Once you've picked someone, let your child help decide what your gift will be. The gift might be a visit, a phone call, or making and sending a card that includes artwork created by your child. It might be a tin of cookies that you bake together, a small basket of vegetables from your garden, or a small bouquet of flowers you pick up at the local flower stand.

7. *Encourage your child to be creative in his giving.* A good gift might be something your child picks up on a vacation—

perhaps a pebble or a piece of driftwood. A gift can also be a framed picture of your child with the person to whom the gift is being given. It can be a gift certificate for service later, such as two free lawn mowings.

One child decided that the best gift he could give to an elderly grandparent in a nursing home was an hour with his dog. After getting permission from the nursing home administrator, he and his father took Poochie to spend some time with Grandma. Grandma truly felt blessed and didn't let Poochie off her lap. In fact, the administrator suggested that the dog be allowed to visit more often.

8. Let your child see you giving to people without regard to their age, gender, race, ethnicity, or nationality. Gifts should flow freely from heart to heart, without regard to any external factor.

Be very careful in choosing gifts that you don't inadvertently choose better gifts for one class or group of people than for others. Granted, those who are close friends or family members are likely to receive gifts more often and of greater value. The caution is in passing on unwanted possessions or buying lesser quality gifts for those who apparently deserve less or need less. Every person deserves a gift of quality.

9. Teach your child how to respond to the gifts he receives. All gifts should be acknowledged with genuine thankfulness. No gift should ever be evaluated for its dollar value. Even if a gift doesn't fit your child, is a duplicate, or doesn't suit his taste, it should still be acknowledged graciously. Teach your child at an early age how to call people and thank them for cards and gifts, and as soon as your child can write, teach him how to write a simple and heartfelt thank-you note.

Pass your bounty on to others. If you receive a present that duplicates something you already have, rewrap it and pass it on to someone you know would appreciate it.

10. Encourage your child to be a generous giver of gifts that have nothing to do with money. Such gifts include compliments, hugs, notes of encouragement, the sharing of Scriptures or positive quotations.

Note that none of these ten lessons is likely to be taught in school. Your child needs to learn them from you, and if you don't teach them, your child may never learn how to be generous.

Also note that these lessons can readily be incorporated into daily life as a family. In teaching your child about giving, your entire family will likely become better givers!

Paying vs. Giving

Make a clear delineation between giving and paying. People pay bills. People buy, sell, and trade on a quid pro quo basis. The expressions "giving a person a deal" or "I'll give you five dollars for it" are not true examples of giving, of course.

A child who has done a set of chores for payment should hear that he has earned it. Thank your child for his effort, and pay him in a straightforward manner just as you would any other employee. Indicate that you are fulfilling an obligation to pay in the amount agreed upon for the work agreed upon. You'll be preparing your child to enter the workforce or sign contracts some day. To reinforce the concept of payment, pay your child separately from giving him his allowance. Don't combine the sums.

Confusion often arises from speaking of "giving" to God's work. Scriptural references to offerings use the words *bring, make,* or *present.* The Old Testament assumes that a percentage of what we have belongs to God and that part of having a covenant relationship with Him is the responsibility to designate the firstfruits of our labor to His work.

That is not to say that giving isn't scriptural. Of course it is! But true gifts in the Bible are those items that are above and beyond basic obligations or commitments.

Explain the distinction to your child. And then when it comes time for her to pass the offering plate at church, she will be ready with a part of her allowance—not a coin that you have slipped to her.

There may be times when your child will benefit from hearing you call a gift what it is—a *gift*. Your child naturally expects clothing, furniture, toys, books, allowance money, and so many other things from you. Your child may not recognize a gift for what it is—a unique and special expression of love that's above and beyond parental responsibility. Point out to your child those things that are gifts.

Sensitivity to Need

Part of developing a generous giving spirit in your child involves helping him or her develop an ability to recognize needs.

Not too long ago I had the opportunity to talk to a college student who had just returned from a missions trip to Mexico. He said, "I had no idea that people could live with so little. And yet, most of the people we met were happy people. They didn't appear to be all that miserable. When it comes right down to it, I guess we really don't need very much if we have enough to eat, a roof over our heads, and people to love." This statement was amazing coming from a young man I knew had a couple of hundred compact discs and at least three dozen shirts!

Genuine needs are very often spiritual and emotional. They're the ones we encounter in the United States most often. Certainly within a radius of fifty miles or less, we can find someone with genuine physical needs; but we all have *daily* contact with emotionally needy people.

These needs don't necessarily require professional help. They're usually garden variety problems: fears, worries, concerns, hurts. We need to teach our children how to identify and address such needs.

There are several ways to help your child become more sensitive to others.

Help your child learn to interpret nonverbal messages. Periodically point out to your child the people around you who have slumped shoulders or a downcast expression. Help your child understand that everybody has problems at least some of the time. Nobody is immune to frustration, hurt, fear, or lack of love.

Help your child identify appropriate responses to the need he perceives. Some children seem to do this intuitively. They're spontaneous and comfortable giving hugs and kisses. Other children don't have a clue how and when to respond.

Another appropriate response is prayer. Include in your prayers mention of those you may have seen during the day but didn't know or couldn't approach.

At other times, your child's most appropriate response is a smile. At still other times, your child can offer a gesture of kindness—taking someone a cold drink, doing an extra chore.

Encourage your child to find a tangible way to help those who are overburdened. Find parts of the load that your child can help carry.

Acknowledging Your Child's Gifts

Be sure you acknowledge the gifts your child gives you. Whether the gift is a daisy from the garden or a note under a magnet on the refrigerator, let him know you appreciate his thoughtfulness.

Talk to your child about how you feel when you have

helped someone; and as your child grows and has experiences of his own, have him share his feelings with you. The good feelings that come from giving must eventually be internalized by your child. That is not something that you can do for him. You are responsible only for setting up situations in which your child can learn the deep inner rewards of giving for himself.

The Rewards of Giving

As a child gives, he is going to receive. That's a basic principle of life. Jesus taught this as recorded in Luke 6:38:

> Give, and it will be given to you: good measure, pressed down, shaken together, and running over will be put into your bosom. For with the same measure that you use, it will be measured back to you.

The more generous your child becomes, the more he will enjoy the gifts of life: rich friendships, honor and respect, lasting relationships. Teach your child to give with an open hand and heart. When God's blessings come back to your child, teach him to receive them with thanksgiving and praise and an increased desire to give even more to those he encounters.

The great reciprocity of the Scriptures is that those who forgive are forgiven. Those who don't judge others aren't judged. Those who refuse to condemn others aren't condemned. And those who give become receivers.

What a good lesson that is to learn . . . and what a privilege it is to teach. The reciprocity extends to parents, too. When you give to your child with a generous, loving spirit, you receive back the loyalty and love of your child. Many a parent would love to have such a gift. Unfortunately, they failed to give it first.

Chapter 8

SIMPLE TRUTH

Lesson #5: Behavior Has Consequences

T he Bible speaks about behavior in fairly black-and-white terms. It's rooted in either sin or righteousness. There's no in between.

While it may be difficult to distinguish them sometimes, the Bible teaches that right and wrong are absolutes. From God's vantage point, judgment is sure. He rewards and punishes impartially, and His nature is unchanging.

God does not mete out one set of punishments or rewards to one group of people and a different set to another group. His commandments and laws are sure.

We do not live, however, in a culture which as a whole recognizes the absolute nature of right and wrong. Laws vary from state to state. Punishment for similar crimes varies from courtroom to courtroom and often according to victim or criminal.

Furthermore, many people in our culture today hold to the opinion that all morality is situational. We simply are who we are, and all behaviors are equally acceptable as long as we don't willfully hurt another person. To hold such a position means each person becomes his own lawmaker. That is a position in sharp contrast to the Bible, which regards all people as being responsible for and accountable to all other people under one objective standard.

In sum, a child isn't going to hear a lot about absolutes or righteousness or sin in the public school classroom. Schools limit themselves to information and achievement, not values and morality. The behavior that has consequence in school is primarily academic. Interrelational misbehavior very often has no consequences or varying consequences. Thus, most parents whose children are in public schools have a great concern about discipline. Schools simply don't know in this day how to discipline effectively and legally, and they lack a moral center for determining which behaviors should be subject to which kinds of rewards and punishments.

There's a significant possibility that your child could go all the way through a public school system today and never hear the words sin or righteousness spoken by a teacher. If the subject of absolutes does come up, it's likely to be couched in these terms: There are no absolutes, and those who believe they exist are people who are attempting to make others feel guilty for not accepting their point of view. Sin and righteousness simply aren't a part of today's school vocabulary.

Even in private schools associated with churches, the same words often go unspoken. Some schools don't want to enter doctrinal debate or present doctrinal positions. Others don't believe it is appropriate for a school to be the setting for a discussion of sin and righteousness—rather that a pastor or preacher should present these concepts from a pulpit. Still others simply don't bring up the subject because they believe the concept of sin might scare children or that the concept of righteousness might not be understood. And still others don't bring up the words because they themselves don't have a working knowledge of these two categories of behavior.

The nature of sin and righteousness—and their consequences—is a lesson that you as a parent are fully responsible for teaching to your child. Your pastor or your child's Sunday school teacher might help, but the primary responsibility is yours.

Working Definitions for Sin and Righteousness

In talking to your child about sin and righteousness, you need to be very precise in your definitions. Earlier in this book, we described information as fact, concept, principle, rule, or procedure. If the Bible is God's definitive word on sin and righteousness, then sin is a:

Fact. Sin exists. It's real. And furthermore, everybody has very intimate experience with it (see Rom. 3:23; 1 John 1:10).

Concept. Sin can be defined and discussed. For our purposes here, let's define sin as a state of being in which a person is separated from God. Because sin is part of our nature, it manifests itself in our behavior.

This may be a different approach to sin from others you've encountered. To many people, sin is something a person does. Behavior, however, must have a motivation. The Bible clearly states that a righteous person does not act in a sinful way, and a sinful person is incapable of acting in a righteous way. (This is a major theme of 1 John.) It is our nature that gives rise to what we say and do. A sinful nature results in sinful behavior; a righteous nature results in righteous behavior.

Principle. The principle of sin is that it is inherent in our human nature and is something that must be renounced as an act of our will.

Rule. Sin has an absolute consequence to it. It kills the soul. Each time an unrepentant person willfully engages in sinful behavior, a piece of his character and potential dies.

Procedure. Sin tends to manifest itself in a pattern that begins with mental deception and ends in overt disobedience.

Why make these distinctions? Because as you talk to your child about sin you must let him or her know if you're talking about humanity's sinful nature, specific sinful behaviors, or the processes of sin. The more precise you are in your discussion, the more fully developed understanding your child will have.

You must also convey that sin and righteousness are opposites. Nor can the two coexist. For a child to recognize sin fully, he must also have a working definition of righteousness. Let me offer a very simple one that a child can easily understand:

Righteousness is having a "right" relationship with your heavenly Father.

I once gave this definition to a group of second graders and then asked them to draw two pictures—one of a sinful person and the other of a righteous person. They were to put God in each picture. One child drew a picture of a girl standing with her arms folded and her back turned to God, who was several feet away, sitting in a big chair. The second picture showed the girl sitting in God's lap with God's arms wrapped around her. I can't imagine a better visual description of sin and righteousness.

Righteousness is also a:

Fact. It is the nature of all who repent of their sins, confess Jesus Christ as God's Son, and acknowledge Him by faith as their personal Savior and Lord.

Concept. It is living in a faith relationship with God and seeking to do only those things that are pleasing to Him.

Principle. When we renounce evil and accept God's gift of Jesus Christ, we receive God's Holy Spirit. It is His Spirit that enables us to live a right-standing life.

Rule. Righteousness results in blessing and eternal life.

Procedure. Righteousness manifests itself through a renewal of the mind, which results in behaviors that are in harmony with God's commandments and laws.

If you are going to talk to your child about the consequences of sin, then you need also to hold out the hope of the consequences of righteousness—a loving relationship with almighty God and the hope of eternal glory!

First Emphasis on Righteousness

Place your foremost emphasis on righteousness.

Make it your first goal as a parent for your child to have a right-standing relationship with God and to live according to His principles on this earth. Nothing else you do as a parent is as important for this life or eternity.

Even a young child is capable of understanding what it means to have a good relationship with someone. Ideally, you have your own relationship with your child as a reference point.

You love your child, regardless of what he or she does. That doesn't mean you approve of all your child's behaviors. Separate actions from value. God loves us no matter what we do. That doesn't mean He loves sinful things we do.

You give to your child those things that are for your child's good. It is an evil parent who does otherwise. God as our heavenly Father wants only good things for us. It is His greatest desire to bless us.

You do your utmost to be present for and available to your child. God is even better at this than you are. God is *always* available to His children.

Young children seem to grasp very easily the concept of sin in terms of a child running away from a good home. Young children generally desire to run away from home because they want to do things their way rather than a parent's way. Runaway children nearly always find themselves alone, miserable, and in danger. The same is true for the person who tries to run away from God's loving presence.

Children also understand the concept of obedience. They know that parents have standards and rules and that the way to avoid punishment is to obey. It doesn't take a great conceptual leap for a child to recognize that God also has rules that must be kept. He doesn't want to make us obey; He wants us to want to obey because we love Him—just as parents hope their children will want to obey more than fear the consequences of disobeying.

I firmly believe that a child is born with an ability to "feel" God, to experience His supernatural presence and power. Unless they live in homes where they are deprived of love or are abused, young children have a wonderful capacity to praise God and to talk to God freely out of their hearts. Encourage your child to do this.

Make your child feel welcome in your church. Don't tuck her away in a nursery or craft class so you can enjoy the service. Include her, and show her how to enjoy the service herself! Your child is not the church of tomorrow. She is part of the church of *today*. If your child has the ability to utter the name of Jesus, your child has the capacity to learn about Him and praise Him.

Include your child in family prayer times. Read Bible stories to him, and as he grows, encourage him to read them aloud to you. Let him listen to Bible stories on tape, watch videos that depict Christ-honoring stories, and listen to audio tapes of praise music. Talk about things you see in terms of how you believe God sees them. Make Jesus a frequent subject of your conversations.

Don't threaten your child with hell or punishment from God's hand. Don't judge your child in God's name. The Lord prefers to do His own judging. In other words, don't instill fear—instill a deep awe of God. Don't allow your child to speak flippantly or irreverently about his heavenly Father.

One of my students once said to me, "My mother always told us that she had put us on the road to heaven and given us a map but that it was up to us to stay on the road and walk out the journey." That young woman had a very wise mother.

Anticipate righteousness as your child's destiny. Give your child a sense of God's divine purpose for her life and assure her that she not only is a beloved creation of God but that God desires to live with her forever.

Assure your child along the way that he doesn't need to be perfect to please God. In fact, the only thing your child truly needs to *do* in life is accept God's love and accept what Jesus did on the cross for him. He doesn't need to work his way to heaven, do endless penance, or live a life without error. We aren't called to crucify ourselves for our sin. We're called only to accept the crucifixion of Jesus as our means of sacrificial redemption.

A Mistake Is Not a Sin

As you talk to your child about sin, make certain that you differentiate among mistakes, errors in judgment, wrongdoing, bad habits, and sin.

Mistakes. Mistakes are generally the result of being in the wrong place at the wrong time. They're not willed or planned. Everybody makes mistakes. They're part of being human, and God made us human beings. We can and should apologize for our mistakes because they often cause harm to others and, in most instances, we should seek to make retribution. But mistakes are not sins before God.

Errors. Errors in judgment are often made because a person hasn't thought things through, has incomplete information, or makes a bad choice *not intending* to cause harm.

Everybody makes judgment errors from time to time. They, too, are part of human nature. We also need to apologize when we make errors and attempt to correct them. But errors are not sins.

Bad habits. We acquire bad habits when we repeatedly do something harmful but don't experience immediate personal harm and nobody tells us we have caused them harm. Numerous behaviors might be classified as bad habits. They can be corrected and, whenever possible, they should be. But bad habits are not necessarily sins.

Wrongdoing. Wrongdoing is just what it says it is: doing wrong. It is doing something to hurt others. It is a willful act—but it doesn't necessarily indicate a pattern of behavior. Wrongful acts tend to be isolated behaviors. They can destroy relationships, and they may be a manifestation of a sinful nature, but they also may be moments of what my grandmother called, "temporary rebellion." Even if we have a righteous nature, we can still choose to act in wrong ways from time to time. This does not mean that we are separated from God as a state of being but that we have momentarily exerted our will in place of His.

Sin. Sin is a pattern of wrongdoing that is deeply rooted in the will. It is a conscious and deliberate choice to be separated from God and to do what a person knows is displeasing to God. It is open and flagrant rebellion.

A student named Ted came over to my home one time, desiring to talk about his relationship with God. Ted was addicted to nicotine. He had smoked for several years, and even though the college rules prohibited smoking on campus, Ted managed to sustain his habit by taking frequent walks and drives off campus.

"My parents are convinced that I'm going to hell because I smoke," he said. "They see tobacco use as a mortal sin. No matter what I say or do, they just don't see how I can have a relationship with God and still smoke."

"Do you and your parents talk about this a lot?" I asked.

"It always seems to come up when I call," he said. "Last week I called them to tell them that I was thinking about going on a missions trip over Easter break, and the first thing my father said was, 'You know you can't smoke on a trip like that.' In nearly every conversation, my mother asks me if I am still smoking the devil's weed."

"Do you want to smoke?" I asked.

"Not really. I've tried to quit three times, but each time I just can't seem to stick with my decision longer than a few days."

"In my opinion, you are engaging in what I would term a bad habit, something that has great potential for causing harm to your own body," I said. "The relationship you have with God and the relationship you have with your parents are two different things, each a separate issue from tobacco use. My greater concern is that you seem to be addicted to a substance to which you don't really want to be addicted. I'd like to see you get free of this habit because I think you'd like to be free of it."

Ted nodded in agreement. Instead of going on the missions trip over Easter break he went to a clinic where he received help for his addiction to nicotine. The last time I talked to him, he hadn't smoked in nearly ten years.

When you criticize your child's behavior, don't call it a sin before God unless you are *very sure* that it is. Much of what a parent punishes or calls to a child's attention are mistakes, errors in judgment, bad habits, and deeds of wrongdoing . . . not sin.

Facing Up to Consequences

In teaching your child that behavior—both good and bad—has consequences, you need to develop a system of rewards and punishments for your child.

Parents often have strict rules about what must *not* be done, with related punishments should certain lines be crossed. They less frequently have rules about what must be done, with related rewards.

Give your child a "to do" list rather than a "don't do" list. And recognize when your child does something right.

Reward your child for the successful completion of chores. Tangible work should be given tangible rewards—even if it's only a star stuck to a chart on the refrigerator door. Bonuses are great for extra effort.

"Intangible" good behavior—such as expressions of truthfulness, patience, and kindness—should be rewarded intangibly, with verbal praise. But never make your love a reward. Your child should always be able to count on it, regardless of his behavior.

If you're linking a reward or punishment to a certain behavior, say so up front. Don't leave your child guessing.

If your child earns a tangible reward, give it in a timely fashion. If your child deserves a compliment, give it immediately. Delayed rewards and punishments are much less effective.

Don't change rules in the middle of a course without a thorough explanation. Be consistent, and don't favor one child over another.

For the most part, rules should be rules, without regard to the situation. If it's wrong to tell a lie, it's wrong to tell a lie. There really are no such things as "white" lies or innocent lies. Falsehood is falsehood.

Don't punish your child in anger. Punish with a purpose—to effect a change in your child's behavior. Too often parents strike out at a child in the heat of the moment. Wait until both you and your child are calm before you exact punishment. The old "count to ten" adage may need to be "count to twenty" or "count to a hundred," depending on your own temperament.

Make certain your child knows what he's being punished for and what his behavior should be. I once overheard a mother say to her young son, "Now, be good."

He replied, "I want to be good, Mommy. But how do I be good?"

Your child needs to know what behavior you expect before you punish him for not doing it!

Don't set your standards too high. Never require perfection from your child. And never expect behavior from your child that he is physically incapable of exhibiting. Don't require, for example, that a four-year-old child sit still for a full hour. It's simply not possible.

Choose punishments that are age-appropriate and meaningful to your child. As much as possible, link those punishments to the nature of the misbehavior. For example, if your child has willfully disobeyed your command not to go out into the street that runs in front of your house, an appropriate punishment would be for him to sit for five minutes facing the fence at the very back of the backyard—which is precisely where your child did not want to be! The teenager who willfully disobeys your request that she clean up her room would be required to clean another area of the house in addition to her room or to polish the copper bottoms on all the kettles in your kitchen.

For a punishment truly to be a punishment, it must not be a cheap penalty. It needs to be perceived by your child as something warranted but unwanted. The parent alone will have to decide where to stand on the issue of spanking. Some children respond to no other form of punishment. Others willingly obey at the sharp tone of voice or a glaring look. It should be something your child wants to avoid and severe enough that he doesn't say, "Wow, that's it? It was worth it!"

After a period of punishment, be sure you reward your

child with praise for good behavior. Let your child know you see the difference and approve of your child's new attitude.

Always assure your child you love him and are punishing him so he will grow up to be a healthy, righteous, and joyful person.

The Rewards of Righteousness

Many parents find punishment much easier to make tangible than reward. Consider these as rewards for your children:

- the privilege of staying up later
- the privilege to make a choice—perhaps to choose the family's Saturday-night entertainment or control the remote control of the television for a couple of hours
- the privilege of doing something without supervision
- the privilege of hosting a party
- the privilege of using something of value (such as driving the family car)

These types of rewards say to a child, "You have earned my trust. You have shown yourself to be a responsible person of good character and judgment."

Don't punish your child if he fails to live up completely to the privilege you just granted him. You may have granted him too much too soon. Scale back your reward next time.

Don't Leave Your Child Guilty

If your child does something you know has hurt someone else, encourage him or her to take these five "A" steps.

Address it. Face the fact that a problem has arisen or a

wrong has been committed. Recognize and acknowledge that something bad has happened.

Admit it. Acknowledge your part in the action that has been hurtful to another person.

Apologize for it. Let the person know you are sorry for what you have done. If you aren't sorry, then you need to face up to that. Face the fact that you don't feel sorrow, admit that this is wrong, and apologize to God for not feeling sorry for hurting another person.

Ask forgiveness. Ask the person to forgive you and to give you a second chance to act in a helpful and positive manner.

Act in a different manner. True repentance involves a change of behavior.

If a child damages someone else's property, a part of your child's apology should include restitution.

If your child comes to you to admit a wrongdoing and ask your forgiveness, be quick to respond and to forgive freely. You will be setting a pattern that your child will intuitively associate with the way God responds to his request for forgiveness.

The most important of the five "A" steps is probably the first one: Address it. If a child doesn't learn to recognize certain behaviors as wrong, he will have no need to take the other four steps. Such a child can easily become prideful and live in a state of denial about his own nature. Rather than tell your child what he has done wrong, from time to time *ask* your child, "What is it that you just did? Was it right or wrong? Why?"

Far more important than punishment or reward is your child's development of his own ability to distinguish between right and wrong behavior. Guilt is a heavy load for any child to bear. Help your child live a guilt-free life by showing him the way out from under guilt's burden: true repentance.

Reinforcing the Consequences of Behavior Displayed at School

Misbehavior at school generally has the following consequences.

- grade reports
- notes sent home from teachers
- trips to the principal's office

As a parent, you will be called upon to respond to these consequences. What should you do when you learn that your child has been sent to the principal's office?

Discuss the situation with your child. Hear your child's version of the story. If it differs from the teacher's story in significant ways, go with your child to the teacher to sort out the truth. Insist that your child face up to the truth of his actions.

Support the teacher's disciplinary action. If a child comes to believe that you will always side with him against a teacher, his behavior is likely to grow much worse in the classroom and he will have less respect for teachers and all people in authority.

Consider disciplinary action of your own. This is especially important if you see a trend extending beyond one teacher or grade level.

If your child brings home a bad grade report, talk to both your child and his teacher about it. Is your child making low grades because he isn't learning or because he's misbehaving or not trying? If the low grades are a matter of inadequate learning, provide your child remedial assistance. You may be able to do it yourself, or you may want to hire a tutor. If the low grades are from inattentiveness, rethink homework and playtime schedules and consider ways you might help your child improve his abilities to concentrate.

And a good report card or praiseworthy note? Post it for the entire family to see. Let your child know that you applaud his success and, more important, you value the effort your child has put into his schoolwork. Let your child know that you are proud of his becoming an eager learner, which is far more important than being a high achiever.

Rejoice with your child over a job well done.

And always, rejoice with your child over his life well lived.

Chapter 9

SIMPLE TRUTH
Lesson #6: Rejoice!

One of the saddest appearing students I ever had was a young freshman named William. I had him in a class for an entire semester and never once saw him smile. If other students greeted him with a smile, he only nodded in return. Will always seemed to have a look I can best describe as downcast.

When Will showed up in one of my classes for a second semester, I invited him over to dinner with a group of other students. After we had eaten, I managed to have a few moments alone with him. I said, "Will, you seem sad much of the time. Are you?"

"Yes, I guess I am," he said. "I wasn't aware that it showed that much."

"Want to talk about it?"

"Well, my mother died, and I guess I haven't found much reason to feel very happy since that happened."

"I'm sorry to hear that," I said.

"Yeah, it happened when I was ten."

"That's a rough age to lose a mom," I said, surprised that he was still showing signs of deep mourning after eight years. "I bet it was a real shock."

"Not really," he said. "She had been sick for a couple of years. We were pretty much expecting her to die."

Again, I was surprised. Most of the time, lingering illness

allows family members to do a significant portion of their grieving prior to the person's death.

"Still, it's hard," I said, trying to empathize. "What did you do to try to get beyond your grief?"

"What do you mean?" he asked.

"Well, there's only so much grieving a person can do," I said. "At least that's my opinion. After a while, you have to get back into life."

"Oh, life went on," he said. "I'm here. I guess I must have done okay in school to get here. I didn't end up in a nut house or anything."

"But what about joy?" I asked. "Life is pretty bland without joy."

"What about joy? I really don't know if I've ever experienced joy. I hear people use that word but frankly, I'm not sure I even know what joy is."

"But you're commanded to have joy," I said to Will, a little surprised at my own statement. That was the first time I had ever said those words.

"What do you mean, commanded to have joy?" Will asked.

"Well, it's the number one commandment in the Bible," I said. "We're told to rejoice more than we're told to do anything else. Rejoice means to express joy. Joy is something we do first, and then the feeling comes."

Will was silent for a few minutes. He seemed to respond to the idea that joy was something a person did, not necessarily something a person felt.

"So how do you *do* joy?" he asked.

"The most important thing, at least in my life, is to praise God," I said, and then added, "and to be very specific about it. No generalizations. Only details."

I picked up a message pad and scribbled this note:
Rx: Joy.

List 100 things to praise God for. Say them aloud each week for the rest of the semester.

I folded the piece of paper and handed it to Will, saying, "I'm making this a class assignment next week, but I thought you might want a head start on it."

As a challenge to myself, I also started a list of things to praise God for. That list was eventually published as a book, *10,000 Things to Praise God For*.

Over the next few weeks, I noticed a subtle change in Will. He actually smiled back when students smiled at him. And then it happened. One of the students gave a hilarious "I Couldn't Believe It" speech and Will actually laughed aloud.

When Will graduated, he was *all* smiles. Still wearing his cap and gown and holding one hand of his bride of two weeks, he found me after the graduation ceremony.

"Thanks," he said, "for teaching me about joy. I don't think Debbie and I would have ever married if I hadn't learned how to see the happy side of life."

One thing I've noticed through the years is that many college students seem to think that *intelligent* means *serious*. They think if you're really smart you know life is just a bag of trouble and there's little to be happy about.

Will made my day—maybe even my whole year. As a teacher, I found a way to tell Will about joy. But don't expect your child to find that lesson as a part of his school curriculum. Our public school system doesn't teach the benefits of having a joyful attitude toward life. If it did, positive-thinking gurus would probably have much smaller audiences.

Joy Is Not the Opposite of Smart

Teachers themselves reinforce this attitude with their statements: Sit down. Be quiet. Pay attention. Don't talk. Don't giggle. Get serious. Even the happiest day of a child's academic career—graduation day—is laden with pomp and circumstance, speeches and ceremony. My urge on a number of occasions has been to shout, "Yippee!" at the top of my lungs—which would not be at all dignified for a person with a doctorate!

If your child is going to learn about joy, he's probably going to have to learn it from you.

The Nature of Joy

Joy is the vocalization of faith. In the Bible, the command to rejoice is very often linked to the phrase "Fear not."

Fear is the true opposite of faith. People who are truly frightened rarely say anything. They curl up in a ball and withdraw emotionally. Fear paralyzes. It keeps a person from risking action and, at times, even reaching out for help. Fear closes off a person to his own potential. It reduces a person's awareness of God. It causes a person to turn inward rather than outward. A frightened person is rarely aware of beauty, goodness, or love.

Faith does just the opposite. It opens a person up to life's wonders and God's glory. It frees a person to engage in relationships, to take risks, to hope, and to explore one's abilities and capacities. It compels a person to move outward and upward. Faith opens up a person truly to see beauty, goodness, and love with new eyes.

The most exuberant expression of faith is joy. The psalmist said it well:

> Make a joyful shout to the LORD, all you lands!
> Serve the LORD with gladness;
> Come before His presence with singing.
> Know that the LORD, He is God;
> It is He who has made us, and not we ourselves;

We are His people and the sheep of His pasture.
Enter into His gates with thanksgiving,
And into His courts with praise.
Be thankful to Him, and bless His name.
For the LORD is good;
His mercy is everlasting,
And His truth endures to all generations
(Ps. 100).

This psalm is a blueprint for joy. One can hardly read it without experiencing joy! I encourage you to use it as a lesson plan for teaching your child how to rejoice.

There are times you need to sing and shout with your child. The songs don't need to be limited to praise songs, but certainly praise songs to God should be included. There are times you need to shout "I love you" across a canyon and hear the words echoing off the hills. There are times when you need to shout in enthusiasm as your child races toward the finish line or rounds the bases after hitting a long fly ball to deep left center. Be free to express your own joy in your child's presence. Invite him to join you.

Psalm 100 says we enter into God's gates with thanksgiving. In Bible times, gates and walls separated homes from a street. *To enter a gate* often meant to enter a small garden or a vestibule where one could wash one's feet before entering a house. To enter a gate meant being safe and accepted.

Along with your child, give frequent expression of thanks for those things that make you feel safe and accepted. Give thanks for your home, your safety, your health, your family, your church, your friends, and everything that provides you a sense of security and identity. Give thanks for the things you see that are beautiful to you—all aspects of God's creation, as well as actions that depict God's grace at work.

When we speak words of genuine thanksgiving, we are

reinforcing our own reliance upon God. We are saying, "I see God as my refuge, the provider of everything I need." When we speak words of thanksgiving, we are also saying, "God has everything in His hands, including the present crisis or problem. I do not need to be afraid. God is in control."

The psalm says that we enter into God's courts with praise. Courts are nearly always linked to royalty. Only certain people have the privilege of entering the court of a king. God is our sovereign King of the universe. As His children, we have access to His court. We are a part of His royal lineage. Our praise focuses on who the King is, what the King has done, and the relationship we have with the King. We praise God, as the psalm says, for:

His lordship. Teach your child that there is only one God. The public school and many private schools will teach children about many gods and the viability of many religions.

His being our creator. Teach your child the simple truth expressed in this psalm: "It is He who has made us, and not we ourselves." Public school will teach your child that he evolved from nothing in an unplanned series of accidents. Many private schools teach the same.

His making us His people. Teach your child that God longs to have a relationship with your child. That's the underlying reason we follow God's rules, go to church, and read the Bible. We are accepting God's invitation to be His people. School places emphasis on individuals, not on groups of people who are committed to one another.

His name. The name of the Lord reflects the complete identity and authority of the Lord. It is His name that He has given to us to use in bringing the good news of healing, deliverance, and salvation to others. Teach your child about the importance of bearing His name into the world. School will teach your child that she is responsible only for her own actions and that she can live in whatever way she wants as long as she keeps secular laws.

His goodness. Teach your child that God is good. The prevailing opinion of the public school is that God is either nonexistent or punitive in nature.

His everlasting mercy. Teach your child about God's abundant capacity and willingness to forgive.

His enduring truth. Teach your child that God not only has a plan for the way we are to live our lives but for all of history. The truth of God lasts. It doesn't change, no matter what humans say or do. School will teach your child that each person is the ruler of his own fate, the master of his own destiny.

Expressions of praise and worship are meant to be voiced. We mustn't just think thankful thoughts or praise God in our minds. There's something mystically wonderful about vocalizing praise. It frees something within us. It gives strength and courage. Be quick to say, "Praise the Lord for ___" and then cite something very specific to your child. Be quick to say, "Oh, I'm so thankful for ___" and cite a specific trait you see.

Be concrete in your expressions of thanksgiving and praise. Point to things your child can see, feel, hear, touch, smell, or taste. In so doing, you will be giving your child an awareness that all good things come from God, *including your child!* Don't neglect to give praise to God for your child's life. Thank God for giving you your child, and do so in front of your child.

The admonition in Psalm 100 to serve the Lord with gladness means we are to do our work as if we were doing it directly for the Lord—for His pleasure. Any task, no matter how mundane, takes on new meaning if we do it as if we were doing it to please the Lord.

Give your child a sense of larger purpose about life's mundane moments. Teach him to see that all work has value and that "serving with gladness" is pleasing to the Lord.

I once heard a mother say to her son, who had just been through a dress rehearsal for a school play the night before and was not amused that he now needed to come off stage and out of the spotlight and rake leaves in the backyard: "Our lives are like a dress rehearsal for heaven. We get to practice here the things that will help us in heaven. Just think—we get to serve the Lord for all eternity. When we learn to serve now, and to do things to the best of our ability, we are just that much better prepared to serve the Lord later."

And then she asked him, "How would you feel if the Lord asked you to zip over to another galaxy and do a chore for Him there?"

"That would be cool," her son said.

"I agree," the mother said. "But how do you suppose the Lord would know He could trust you to do that for Him?"

"I don't know," the boy replied.

"Well I think He'll know that in part because He sees that you are able to do chores now and do them well. Why don't you imagine that these leaves are on another planet and that the Lord has asked you to rake them? You'll have a much better time if you get into that attitude."

The boy followed his mother's advice, and through the kitchen window, we watched him rake up a storm. He came in smiling about a half hour later.

"Next galaxy?" he said with a big grin.

Not Just a Happy Face

True joy is not just a matter of putting on a happy face. One can think positively and not have a relationship with God. True joy flows from the deepest recesses of the heart. It is not situational or circumstantial. It is a part of a person's very soul.

When your child comes to you looking dejected, expressing sorrow, or feeling down in the dumps, hear him out. Let him tell you about the situation that has made him feel sad or disappointed. There's healing therapy in giving your child an opportunity to express his pain.

Don't deny the importance of pain. Don't dismiss lightly the feelings that your child is expressing. All emotions are valid ones. What we feel, we are wise to express (albeit in ways that are appropriate and beneficial). Never say to your child, "Oh, that's nothing" or "That doesn't matter" or "You'll feel better tomorrow."

Two of the greatest lies parents tell their children are "Time will heal," and "Things will get better." Time doesn't heal anything. It may cause a memory to fade a little, but some of the most bitter and resentful people I know had bad things happen to them twenty, thirty, and even forty years ago. Things don't necessarily get better. Sometimes they get worse.

A much better approach is to say, "Let's talk to God about this." Let your child tell God in your hearing about how he feels. And after your child ends his prayer, say, "Now, let's praise the Lord for giving us the courage to go on in life." Take turns voicing sentences of praise.

Verbal expressions about God bring about a change of feeling deep within the soul. A forced smile doesn't do that.

Instilling Curiosity and Building a Desire to Relate

The more your child focuses on God's goodness, the more he will come to see that this world is a wonderful place filled with wonderful people.

This isn't a Pollyanna perspective. It's a truthful and realistic look at life. The good side to life far outweighs the bad. Most people manifest good behavior. There's something good your child can learn from nearly everybody.

Goodness is attractive. We all want to be around people who are happy. Nearly every person responds intuitively to beauty. When we see the world as being good, we're more likely to want to explore it. Therein lies curiosity at its best.

When we see life as an opportunity and not a burden, we're more likely to look for new ways of expressing ourselves. Therein lies creativity.

Curiosity and creativity are two of the greatest traits you can encourage in your child, especially when it comes to your child's intellectual pursuits. The child who is bound up with fear is far less likely to express curiosity or creativity.

The child who sees people as having wonderful qualities is much more likely to expect the best from others and get it. I don't mean, of course, that you shouldn't warn your child about evil people or teach him to be cautious with strangers. But do encourage your child to ask questions and weigh a person's responses.

There's a difference between being good and having good qualities. Teach your child that people have good to offer and a capacity to do good things. God alone knows how good a person truly is. We human beings are in a position, however, to do good things for each other and relate in good ways.

Again, these lessons are best taught by their being "caught." Your child will learn most of what he learns about praise, thanksgiving, serving with gladness, curiosity, creativity, and an open stance toward others by watching you in action.

As you praise God and give expressions of thanksgiving, your child will learn how to praise and express thanksgiving. As you relate to others in an open, honest way so will your child. As you serve with gladness, doing your work in life as if you are working directly with the Lord, so your child will come to see that all work is best done with an attitude of service to God. As you sing, your child will learn your songs. As you shout with joy, your child will learn to shout with joy. As you express yourself creatively, your child will try to find unusual ways of expressing himself, too. And as you express a curiosity about the unknowns of life, your child will find his own curiosity piqued. To that end, the best thing you can do is adopt a stance of "there's more to learn." We turn next to that simple lesson.

Chapter 10

SIMPLE TRUTH
Lesson #7: Keep Learning

One of my favorite colleagues in college was a woman more than forty years older than I. Frances had taken two years of teacher's training back in the 1920s and then had taught public school music classes for a few years prior to her marriage. When her husband later retired from a publishing firm and went to work part-time at the university where I was enrolled, Frances decided to go back to college.

Initially, she intended to get a degree but she soon discovered that she had no interest in having test anxiety in her sixties. Neither was she interested in writing lengthy term papers. Her main interest was in reading and attending lectures, so she audited classes.

Over the next twenty years (long after I graduated), she accumulated more than 140 hours of audit credits. We stayed in close contact through those years. The last time we did a tally, she had taken eight semesters of Shakespeare and six semesters of music appreciation. Why? Because she found something new to read, hear, and learn each time she took a course. And besides, in her words, "The teachers and students are different each time, so the discussions are different."

Frances not only loved to take classes at the university. She was an avid member of the Tuesday Book Club, which met monthly to discuss new books on the market, and she and her husband were ardent supporters of the symphony and the opera in our city.

Frances was still very young at heart and agile in mind when she died a few years ago. She was a great inspiration to me of a simple truth all parents need to teach their children: Never stop learning.

Learning Comes in Many Packages

Learning happens in a wide variety of ways. Formal instruction in a classroom setting is only one of them.

There are two main ways you can help your child understand the importance of continual learning:

- Model that behavior in your own life.
- Give your child an opportunity to have learning experiences that are not school-bound.

To model continuous learning, you can take a course, make a course, and read, read, read.

Take a course. Colleges these days have a number of options for continuing education students (even those who have never attended college before). There are night, weekend, and summer courses; abbreviated seminar classes which sometimes last only a few weeks but require many hours each day or evening; and correspondence courses. Independent-study courses can usually be arranged, in which a student works with a professor to define a course by choosing books, experiences, and evaluation techniques unique to the subject.

The course you take might be one offered at your church. Many churches these days have Bible-training institutes, a Lenten series of classes, or short courses (sometimes just three or four weeks) that focus on a particular topic or spiritual practice.

Communities often have classes under the banner of open university or neighborhood school. These courses are sometimes arranged by the city's department of parks and recreation. The courses tend to vary widely, from macrame to poetry reading.

Galleries and performing arts centers often have series of concerts, plays, and other performances that include discussion afterward. Travel series and lecture series are sometimes available, sponsored corporately or by nonprofit agencies. The YMCA and YWCA offer classes in many communities.

If you haven't finished high school, do so. It will be a good example to your child that you value a high school degree "for real," and not just in theory or lip service. And your child will be much more inclined to do his homework if you two are both doing homework at the same time.

Make a course. If you aren't inclined to take a course that has been structured by someone else, consider structuring your own course. I have a friend who goes to a family vacation home for several weeks a summer, and each year she studies something new. For several months she gathers as many tapes, books, and magazine articles she can find on a particular subject of interest and then immerses herself in the short course of her own design while sitting on her deck overlooking the lake.

Another friend has a long-standing interest in archaeology and ancient civilizations. She has never been on an archaeological dig, but she has read countless volumes on the subject, both fiction and nonfiction, over the last ten years.

A systematic course of study sends a signal to your child that learning in any one discipline can go on as long as you like.

Read regularly. My mother "always had a book going." In fact, she always had several books partially read. Reading was her favorite pastime. Our home was filled with books—fiction, nonfiction, reference materials. When I was in elementary school, one of my teachers asked us to count the books in our home and bring the total to school the next day. When I came in with a total of more than five hundred books, she sent a note home apologizing to my mother for the time it must have taken us to count them all. She had not expected any of her students to report more than forty or fifty books.

In addition to books, Mother subscribed to a good number of magazines, including journals related to my father's business. When my parents weren't reading the newspaper or a book, they were probably reading a magazine.

Your child will see much more value in reading quality instructional material if he sees you reading material that is substantive.

Share Learning Experiences

Apart from watching you, your child can gain a great deal by sharing educational experiences with you. Here are five activities or experiences you both are likely to find very enjoyable.

Travel. We discussed the value of travel earlier, but it cannot be overemphasized. Travel opens your child to untold possibilities, as well as builds self-esteem. Especially as your child enters her teen years, consider going on tours as a family. Choose one that includes cultural or educational components—such as concerts, visits to galleries or museums, and visits to historical sites.

As you plan your own family vacations, include educational activities. In our family travels, we have been to one particular city on a number of occasions. Each time, we visited at least one major gallery, museum, or historical site we hadn't seen before. On our regular summer travels by car, we regularly stopped at historical markers by the roadside to read their inscriptions or took the time to visit cultural or historical sites as a part of each journey.

Cultural events. Check out the plays and concerts coming up in your city and pick a few you can go to as a family. Some symphony orchestras and theater companies have cultural series especially for children. As your child enters the teen years, take him to a full-fledged adult symphony concert, a ballet, an opera, and a play or musical. Study a little about the music or play in advance. Make the evening a special one, perhaps with dinner out before the performance or a special dessert afterward. The event likely will be an experience your child will never forget.

A number of cities have specialized events, such as Mayfest or Reggaefest or Oktoberfest. In some places, a particular composer or author is featured, such as Shakespeare or Mozart. As you travel, be aware of these unique opportunities to expose your child to a particular style of music or dramatic presentation that may not be available in your own city.

Local galleries and museums. Introduce your child at least once to each major gallery or museum in your city or in the city closest to you. Take advantage of a general tour to introduce your child to what a gallery or museum is all about. And then take in the special exhibits that are offered from time to time.

A growing number of museums and galleries have special exhibits of interest to children or sections of the building designed specifically for children. Many museums have hands-on experiential or experimental displays in which children can manipulate devices or conduct mini-experiments. Take advantage of these unique opportunities to introduce your child to lessons in art and science that he may not have had in school.

A museum of interest can even include the museum at

the Indianapolis Speedway or a national hall of fame featuring a particular sport or type of music.

Science exhibits. Children love to go to zoos and aquariums. They're fascinated by planetariums. Botanical gardens are a great way to kindle an interest in gardening. If you are a city dweller, you might want to explore the possibility of taking a family excursion to a working farm or ranch. A growing number of places offer weekend and weeklong stays.

As you travel, be aware that nearly all of the national parks and many of the national forests, as well as state parks and forests, have special media or lecture programs that cover the geology, flora, and fauna of the region. A number of places that have been built now as replicas of past times—for example, Plimoth Plantation outside Boston and Williamsburg in Virginia—are fully operating today.

Instructional television programs and videos. Don't let your child get by with watching only entertainment videos. Bring home a few that expose your child to performances of well-known plays and concerts, science programs, and world travel. If you can't travel or take in cultural experiences with your child, at least be armchair travelers and theater goers. Sit down and watch the programs with your child. Talk about what you have seen.

Give Your Child Lessons and Camps

As soon as your child is old enough to practice, let her begin lessons of her choice. You may want to set parameters, of course. For example, you may see great value in music lessons. It's important for a child to learn to read music and play an instrument. The value extends far beyond music itself to eye-hand coordination, creativity, cultural awareness, respect for private instruction, and the discipline of practice. A parent can give a child a choice, however, as to the instrument he wants to play.

Have two simple time rules for lessons: Your child must take them for an agreed upon period of time and practice daily for a set amount of time. Then stick with the rule. Twenty minutes a day is a good minimum. Going beyond forty-five minutes a day for an elementary school child will probably result in burnout. Two thirty-minute sessions may be acceptable, however, if your child happens to be taking instruction in two instruments at the same time. Daily practice is the only way your child will make enough progress from week to week to stay encouraged and motivated.

You may want to encourage your child to take lessons in other areas.

Dance lessons
Art lessons
Sports lessons

If your child wishes to continue taking lessons in a particular field after an initial round of study, consider letting him help pay part of the expenses. Your child will value the lessons more.

Camps. Numerous types of camps are available for children and teens. Sports camps are often held on college campuses. Many cities offer day-camp opportunities, generally with a full menu of courses to take. A growing number of symposiums and conferences are held for teens, sometimes in specialized areas such as medicine or the environment. A few travel tours are available, too, for teens. These generally emphasize historical sites, national monuments, or natural wonders.

Library reading clubs. Many libraries have summer programs that encourage students to read. Some of the programs include book reviews or book parties with well-known authors. Others feature movies based on classic children's stories. Some offer prizes for the students who read the most books. Check out the possibilities at your library!

Teamwork. You may think Little League is just for fun, but participation on sports teams can be very educational. Encourage your child to keep stats on his performance, as well as overall team performance. (These are actually math exercises in disguise.) Check out instructional videos on the sport. Attend professional games if possible. Talk about the histories of various teams. Make sure your child warms up properly to avoid early injuries and that he uses prescribed safety equipment. Participation in team sports can provide a good introduction to the subjects of anatomy, physiology, and nutrition.

Summer school. Summer is an excellent time for your child to catch up in remedial studies. Summer school is also a great way to take courses that aren't offered in the fall or to get a required course out of the way so he can take an elective instead.

Some college campuses offer summer school courses geared toward helping high school students gain the study skill and prerequisite information and skills (especially in reading and writing) that are necessary to college success.

Part-time work. A job is a wonderful learning experience! A teen of fifteen should be encouraged to get a summer job if at all possible. She'll enjoy earning money and probably gain a new appreciation for both work and the need to manage money wisely. If your child shows an interest in a particular career field, do what you can to help her get an internship in that field, even if the position is a nonpaying one.

Self-study. Encourage your child to pursue individual interests. He may want to take on a 4-H project or prepare something for next year's county fair. Perhaps he'd benefit from having a microscope of his own, along with books and other tools to help him explore the world of his own backyard. Let your child develop his own summer course of study. He may want to specialize in a particular author, subject, or type of literature.

Make It Fun!

Sounds like a lot of fun, right? Learning is fun. Keep it that way for your child.

Your child is in school only about half the days in each year. On the calendar it stretches over nine months but, in reality, it's only about one hundred and eighty days.

The other half of the year is a blank agenda on which you can plan numerous experiences to broaden your child's horizons and spawn a new interest.

Certainly, not all of the above suggestions should be implemented in any one year. Pick and choose. Find a new instructional focus for each summer, depending on your child's interests.

Learning About Other People

So far this chapter has focused on topical learning. You can also enhance your child's desire to "always keep learning" about people.

Invite people into your home; go to places where your child can meet people from different walks of life and different races and cultures.

Some churches have close ethnic ties. One Greek Orthodox church regularly sponsors dinners to which the public is invited. These are great times to introduce children to Greek food, music, and customs. Some neighborhoods or towns sponsor ethnic festivals because the people in those towns are of one main ethnic group. Take your child along as you explore a new culture.

If you have friends of other races or cultures, invite them

over for an evening of dinner and conversation. Let your children ask questions. You many want to prepare them in advance for any unusual customs that your friend observes or items of clothing that your friend wears. Suggest questions they might ask to gain more information about your friend's culture.

The same goes for friends who may work in occupations other than your own or for friends who have recently been to a foreign country. Invite them over to share their travels or to tell what it was like to live and work in another country. Again, suggest questions your child might ask about the work your friend does.

Take your child to work with you a day or two a year. (Be sure to get your employer's permission first.) Let her see you in action and discover firsthand what Mom or Dad does all day. Let your child see you interacting with others and operating the machines or using the equipment that you normally use. Give her a task to do so that she feels as if she has worked, too. You may even consider paying her privately for the day's work.

Learning More About Yourself

One of the most important lessons you can help your child learn is that he is interesting and talented.

Schools give four types of tests to try to determine what a child is like.

Readiness tests. Usually administered to preschoolers, these tests determine if a child is ready for kindergarten. They are especially common in private schools. I suggest that, if at all possible, a parent avoid these tests like the plague. They rarely yield information that is helpful to your child, in part because children at age four or five are learning very quickly and in spurts. What a child doesn't know at the time he takes the test, he may very well know two weeks later. These tests are often used to segregate children along socioeconomic lines and to put children into certain "tracks." Don't let your child be labeled or pigeonholed that early in life if you can avoid it.

Intelligence tests. These are commonly known as IQ tests, IQ referring to "intelligence quotient." These tests were originally designed to measure a child's *capacity* for learning. They're helpful, in my opinion, as a snapshot of a child's potential on any given day. They can also help isolate a particular area of weakness or dysfunction. Keep in mind, however, that IQ test scores for individual students have varied as much as twenty or thirty points or more, in a twelve-month period. That amount of variance can be the difference between retardation and average intelligence or average intelligence and genius! By and large, IQ scores are not correlated to a child's ability to achieve good grades or get a good job later in life. They are totally unrelated to a child's ability to socialize, make sound judgments, or develop the life skills discussed in Chapter 5. What they can do is discourage a child or cause a child to feel proud. They often skew a teacher's perception to expect less or more from a child. My advice is to pay very little attention to them, and don't panic if your child doesn't score where you think he or she should.

Achievement tests. These tests are usually given annually through elementary school. The purpose is to note both individual understanding of the prescribed curriculum for that year and, more commonly, to obtain averages of student performance for any one teacher or school. They're normalized tests, which means that your child's performance is measured against all other students taking the exam in the test field (which is generally your state). The results measure where a child stands in terms of percentile—the higher the percentile, the better a child performed in comparison to other students. The tests often do not tell what percentage of the actual questions were scored correctly, only how the child compares to other test takers. These tests are most helpful to individual teachers, including parents who are home schooling. Teachers can see how their students as a class are doing compared to other classrooms of students. That depicts a certain quality of instruction. The tests have very little benefit directly to the individual student as far as predicting future school success.

College-entrance tests. These tests, generally speaking, the SAT (Scholastic Achievement Test) or ACT (American College Test), are used by colleges to set standards for admission and financial aid. Because of that, they can be important to your child's future. I suggest that you help your child prepare for these tests through a self-study book, a computer self-study program, or a course. It is also helpful to have your teen take the Pre-SAT if possible and the SAT or ACT early enough to take it again if he scores low. The tests are used to weed people out of quality programs, and you want to do what you can as a parent to keep your child's options from being limited.

Unfortunately, these tests are not a very accurate predictor of overall college success. Too many other variables come into play. Their main benefit to the colleges is that they tend to neutralize or give a second opinion to a student's grade point average. Colleges have virtually no way of knowing whether a student earned his grades in a tough or lenient academic environment. A 3.0 average from a school with high academic standards might reflect greater effort and knowledge than a 3.5 average from a mediocre school.

These tests do give a student an indication as to how adept he is at taking multiple-choice exams, which can be important to know since most college tests fall into that category.

Although not highly helpful to your individual child, these tests are a fact of life and they do pigeonhole your college-bound student, whether you like it or not. Help your child do his best on the tests, and once they're over and he's in college, suggest that he forget his score.

You will note that none of these tests is of great benefit *to your child*. There are tests, however, which can be beneficial.

Aptitude tests. The aptitude test isolates your child's unique talents. Keep in mind that an aptitude is an ability. The Johnson O'Connor tests are probably the most complete, but they are also among the most expensive. Very often you will need to find a psychologist or counselor who offers psychometric testing in order to locate these tests. As far as I am concerned, however, they're worth their weight in gold.

A child who takes a good aptitude test comes away with an understanding that he is truly gifted in some way—a measurable, observable way—and in that, a child feels valued. Children who take aptitude tests have greater direction in life. They are able to aim their talents toward particular goals, and because they're operating within their gifts, they have a greater likelihood of reaching those goals. This adds further to self-esteem. The tests can also help a child find a career path that has the greatest potential for fulfillment and joy.

Career planning tests. These are sometimes labeled as aptitude tests, but they're not based on your child's abilities so much as they are on your child's interests. They're a series of questions aimed at determining the specific things your child finds enjoyable. Based upon the results, various career options are suggested. These tests are most useful to a child who has already taken a good aptitude test. Coupling one's innate capabilities with one's interests can be a very good formula for career success later in life! In a very practical way they can help a child zero in on a college major very quickly, eliminating much confusion and saving tuition dollars.

Personality tests. As your child enters his teen years, you may want to explore the possibility of taking a personality test together. Make sure you also take any follow-up instruction associated with the test. Otherwise, it's too easy to jump to conclusions that may not be valid. The Myers-Briggs test is one that many people have found helpful.

The Enneagram is another psychological model that is gaining favor today. It has been used for centuries in spiritual communities and for the past twenty years has been featured in many Roman Catholic retreats. A growing number of psychologists are using it in their practices as well. The Enneagram identifies nine major personality types in a wheel configuration. A person is helped to identify his primary spoke of the wheel and also the wing positions on either side of the primary spoke.

Both the Myers-Briggs test and the Enneagram have been linked to career options, the premise being that a person should find a job that is in keeping with his or her personality.

I favor combining all three approaches. Find out what you are equipped to do (aptitude testing). Take a look at who you are in terms of personality traits. And then explore what it is that you like to do (career testing). The person who goes into a field of study knowing her innate gifts and basic tendencies is more likely to succeed.

An Appreciation for Uniqueness and Similarities

Teach your child that he is a unique creation. Don't let your child feel that any of these tests limits him. Tests may put your child into groups, but he is unique, unlike any other person, in his genetic profile, personal history, and potential for creative expression. No other person has his precise combination of abilities and talents. Your child's destiny is unique.

As your child takes these tests, he is likely to benefit from something of a side effect: greater tolerance for others.

Children often see people in two categories—those they like and those they don't. Aptitude and personality tests, especially, point out to your child that people are different, not necessarily good or bad. A person who is a "number one" on the Enneagram may not have a great deal in common with a "number five" in personality, but both can see better why they act as they do. A person who scores as an "introvert" on the Myers-Briggs test may not like being around an "extrovert" all the time, but he probably has a greater understanding of the extroverts he encounters in his daily life.

These tests present the possibility that as your child learns more about himself he will also learn more about others and how to relate to them.

Why should you take the test with your teen? Because in all likelihood, the two of you will score differently! Parents often expect their children to be just as they are—to have all of the same personality traits, interests, and abilities. Sometimes they're disappointed when they discover this is rarely true. By taking these tests together, *you* will discover to a greater extent the uniqueness of your own child. And your child will have a better understanding of why you make certain decisions or respond in certain ways as a parent.

I'm certainly not advocating that the two of you psychoanalyze each other. Rather, I'm suggesting you gain a new appreciation for your similarities and differences, and that you grow in your understanding of each other.

A Balanced Process

A person can continue to discover more about other people and himself all his life. Teach your child to pursue a balance. The person who studies only himself is going to become a self-absorbed, dysfunctional bore. The person who studies only content is going to become a reclusive specialist who has little ability to relate to others. The person who pursues only a knowledge of other people isn't likely to have much to talk to them about and may feel unnecessary pain when others aren't as keen to build a relationship in return.

Keep learning new things.

Keep meeting new people.

Keep learning more about yourself.

And as you do, share what you're learning with your child. Talk to your child about your new discoveries and how you hope to apply them to your life in a positive way.

Encourage your child to learn new things, meet new people, and explore more of his own personality and potential. Invite him to share with you what he's learning.

You will become colleagues in learning.

Chapter 11

SIMPLE TRUTH

Lesson #8: Forgive Generously

I once assigned a class of students to write a one-page description entitled "My Best Friend." The students were to use as many descriptive adjectives and adverbs as possible and also tell how they met their friend and on what they felt their friendship was based. I admonished them, "Let me feel as if I really know your friend."

One of the students, Linda, surprised me. She wrote, "Michelle is my best friend today, but five years ago she was my worst enemy. I love her now. I hated her then." And then she proceeded to describe Michelle and her relationship with Michelle in very clear and creative ways. Linda never did tell me, however, how it was that Michelle went from being an enemy to being a friend. I was curious and invited Linda and two other students to join me for lunch.

There, Linda told me how she and Michelle had been rivals in school—rivals in earning grades, attracting boyfriends, entering contests, earning "chairs" in band (both played clarinet), and pursuing various honors. "We sort of traded wins," Linda said.

"You considered her to be an enemy?" I asked.

"Not an enemy in terms that I wanted to destroy her, but yes, an enemy in terms that I wanted to beat her."

"What happened?" I asked.

"I had a dream," Linda said. "And in my dream, Michelle

was in danger. I was the only one who could figure out how to rescue her . . . and I did. It felt really good. When I awoke, for some reason I had a knowing that my hatred of Michelle wasn't right and that God wasn't pleased about it."

"Did you say anything to Michelle?" I asked.

She said, "I didn't tell her about my dream for several years. What I did was call her and tell her that I was sorry I had been mean to her on occasion. She was really nice, and she also apologized to me. Before the conversation ended, we were laughing together. After that, we were friendlier to each other, and then the day came when the school announced a music competition for ensembles. In addition to the clarinet, Michelle and I both played the piano. I called her and suggested that we enter together. And she suggested that we do a clarinet piece that had two movements—she would accompany me on the piano for the first movement and then we'd quickly switch places and I'd accompany her on the second movement. We won, hands down. And from that time on, we were friends."

"Did you still compete?" I asked.

"Not really. We both tried out for a few of the same things in high school, but when that happened, we agreed ahead of time that it didn't matter which one of us won as long as one of us did. A few times we decided to try for different things. One year she was class secretary and I was vice president."

"And now?" I asked.

"I call her about twice a month. She's at another college, and we have a great time comparing notes. We're both doing great. One of the things Michelle and I realized is that we probably wouldn't have competed with each other so fiercely if we hadn't had so much in common."

"How did your parents feel about the rivalry between the two of you?" I asked.

"My mother hated it, and so did Michelle's mother, I think. Whenever I'd say something negative about Michelle in those early years, Mom would say, 'She's not your real enemy.' I never really knew what Mom meant until much later. Michelle really wasn't my enemy. I was my own worst enemy for having such an intense need to win at any cost."

In many ways, what Linda and Michelle did was to forgive each other.

Forgiveness Means Letting Go and Trusting God

The term *forgiveness* has been used several times in previous chapters. The forgiveness we are talking about in this chapter doesn't relate to the divine forgiveness that a person experiences from God but, rather, the forgiveness we extend to others.

Forgiveness means letting go—no longer keeping another person within a prison of hatred in our hearts.

Forgiveness does not mean we're denying that an offense has occurred or that we are at odds with another person. Forgiveness is not denial.

Forgiveness is not saying, "It didn't matter," or "It was unimportant." Forgiveness is not a cover-up.

Forgiving is not the same as forgetting. The old saying "forgive and forget" hardly ever works completely. We can probably never forget offenses fully but we *can* forget that they *mattered*. We can say, "I choose to forgive and not let the memory of this stand in my way or cloud my future." We can ask the Lord to help us forget the hurt we feel.

Forgiveness is saying, "I will no longer hold on to this resentment. I choose by an act of my will to let it go and to trust God for two things. First, that God will heal my heart and replace my loss. And second, that God will deal with the person who has offended me in the way He sees fit."

When we forgive, three things happen.

We put ourselves in a position to be forgiven. Jesus taught this as recorded in Luke 6:37, "Forgive, and you will be forgiven." He also said, "If you forgive men their trespasses, your heavenly Father will also forgive you. But if you do not forgive men their trespasses, neither will your Father forgive your trespasses" (Matt. 6:14–15). Those are sobering words.

We find that we are no longer blinded by hate but are able to see the truth. Hate compels a person only to see the bad attributes of another person. The truth is that each person is a mixture of both good and bad attributes. When we see the truth about another person, we're forced to see the good attributes. In so doing, we also find ourselves in a position better to see the truth about ourselves: that we have both faults and positive attributes, too.

We're able to ask for forgiveness. When that happens, true healing and reconciliation can occur. Enemies can become friends.

At the very core of the ability to forgive lies the potential for living in peace.

I have yet to meet a parent who *longs* for his child to hate others. All but the most evil of parents want their children to live in peace and to have healthy, loving, peaceful relationships.

And schools don't teach this. Oh, they teach about the need for peace, usually in the context of sociology. But they rarely teach a person *how* one individual might turn an enemy into a friend.

On the contrary, schools promote competition, which so readily leads to hatred and revenge. Schools have rival sports teams. Students compete for grades and awards. From the earliest grade levels, children are put into groups on the basis of ability, and distinctions are made between the "smart kids" and the "dumb kids." Scholarships and entrance into certain programs is granted frequently as a result of competition. In the main, the classroom and the school system is a very competitive place. The same goes for the playground. Almost all sports are rooted in competition, either team or individual.

I'm not saying that all competition is bad. Competition has its place. The best form of competition is when a student competes against his own best previous mark, not when he competes against another person.

The insidiousness of competition is that it results in winners and losers, and a healthy person doesn't intuitively like to lose. A loss is just that—less: less prestige, less power, less acceptance, less reputation, less esteem. The normal tendency is for a person who has lost to want to compete again, try harder, do better, and beat the other person. If a person continually loses, that person is likely to become bitter and vengeful. At that point, hatred sets in. And hatred often erupts into violence and aberrant behavior.

Your child is going to learn a great deal about competition in school but not a lot about the benefits of genuine cooperation and friendship or the forgiveness that enables two people to be friends. He'll have to learn that lesson from you.

Teaching Your Child to Forgive

There are four distinct things you can do to help your child forgive others and live in an attitude of inner freedom and peace.

1. Model forgiving behavior to your child. Your most effective means of teaching your child to forgive is for *you* to forgive others freely. Don't hold grudges or exact revenge. Don't speak ill of other people or express a desire to see them fail. Let your child hear you ask forgiveness of others. Let him overhear you asking God to help you forgive those who wrong you.

2. Insist that your child forgive others who wrong him. "Forgive, so that you might be forgiven" is not a nice platitude. It's a command. You have the authority as a parent to insist that your young child obey it. Let your child know that *you* know that he has been hurt. Agree with her that the other person shouldn't have done what he did and that you consider this to be an important matter.

Then, encourage your child to join you in praying for the person who has wronged her: "Heavenly Father, please help me to forgive this person and not hold it against him. Help me forget the way I feel about this. I trust You, heavenly Father, to deal with this person. Please help me see this person as being Your child and to find an opportunity in the near future to be better friends with this person."

After your child has prayed this type of prayer, don't allow her to exact revenge or seek to undermine the other person.

3. Don't use the past as an excuse. Let the past lie in the past. Don't dredge it up as an excuse for your current troubles.

Marty was a student of mine who couldn't let go of her past. She was one of the most angry and bitter young women I've ever met. She was very vocal in talking about the wrongs she felt had been done to her by her parents and grandparents. As best I could tell from what she said, her parents had not abused her physically, emotionally, or sexually. What they had done was require that Marty keep the rules of their home, which included a strict curfew and a restricted set of friends. Marty deeply resented the fact that her parents had not allowed her to stay out late at night, go to the parties she desired to attend, or go on certain trips that her friends had planned to the lake or beach. She blamed her current lack of friends and boyfriends on what her parents had done. "They turned me into some kind of a nun," she said.

One evening another student, Phil, provoked Marty's

anger to a peak. He openly declared that he had heard enough of Marty's complaining about her past. He confronted her on a retreat that I was chaperoning. In a kind but very firm way, Phil said, "Marty, I wish you would quit using your parents as an excuse."

"They are an excuse," she flared with venom in her voice.

"No," Phil said, "they aren't. They did what they thought was best and you rebelled against their rules. It's your rebellious spirit that keeps you from having friends and boyfriends now, not what your parents did."

Marty grew very quiet and crossed her arms as if to block out what Phil was saying. He persisted. "When I first met you, I wanted to ask you out, Marty, but then I heard you talk about your parents and you were so angry and bitter I thought, *I don't know if I want to get involved with this girl or not. All she wants to talk about is her parents and how they've done her wrong. If I date her and then we break up, she'll probably say the same things about me and blame me for her problems. I don't need that.*"

"I wouldn't have done that," Marty said defensively.

"How was I to know?" Phil said. "I think you need to forgive your parents for whatever it is you think they did to you, and then go on with your life. Make your own decisions. They aren't in control of your life now unless you let them be in control . . . in your mind."

Marty didn't respond, and the conversation took a different turn. Marty remained angry for several more months, and then one day it was as if a light was turned on inside her. Her very countenance was different. I saw her in the foyer of our office suite and asked her, "What has happened to you, Marty?"

"What do you mean?" she asked.

"You look different," I said. "There's a glow I haven't seen before."

She said, "Well, do you remember that retreat?"

"Yes," I said.

"Do you remember what Phil said?"

"Yes."

"Well, I finally asked God to forgive me for the way I've been acting—you know, about my parents. And I called them and asked them to forgive me. They cried and I cried. And I guess all those tears just turned into a glow."

They certainly did. How I wish more young people could forgive their parents for the things they think their parents have done to them. Most parents act in good faith toward their children. If they knew they were making parenting mistakes, they wouldn't make them. But all parents fail their children at certain points.

You probably can't *tell* your child this in a way that will be meaningful to him while he is still a child, but you can refuse to use your own parents as an excuse. And some day, when your child is a young adult, you can ask your child to forgive you for mistakes you may have made as a parent.

If you use the past as an excuse, you never fully face up to the real reason for failures in your life. The same holds true for your child. On the other hand, when a person faces up to failure in an honest way, he nearly always can find a way to overcome it. Letting the past be responsible may be convenient or comfortable, but it doesn't result in a change for the better. Facing today's failures head-on and then moving forward to try solutions is a formula for growth.

4. Don't let yourself become a victim of shame or make your child a victim of shame. Never say to your child, "Shame on you," or "You have brought shame on our family." Those are two of the worst statements a parent can ever make to a child. Shame is a feeling that you have been marked with some kind of indelible ink so that no matter what you do your past wrong remains obvious to others. Shame concludes that a person can never be fully forgiven. It is an act of judgment and condemnation. It declares that a person is not worthy of God's love and therefore is less worthy of human love.

The Bible stands in strong opposition to us as human beings taking judgment and condemnation in our own hands. In the same passage in which Jesus is recorded as teaching about forgiveness we find these words: "Judge not, and you shall not be judged. Condemn not, and you shall not be condemned" (Luke 6:37).

If you feel shame about something in your past, recognize that it is a lie. The enemy of your soul has tried to convince you that you have done something that can never be forgiven on earth or in heaven. That is not what the Bible teaches. The Bible's approach is that "if we confess our sins, He is faithful and just to forgive us our sins and to cleanse us from all unrighteousness" (1 John 1:9).

God's desire is that you be free of shame and that your child never know its stain.

Looking to a Better Day

In letting go of the past and holding no ill feelings toward another person, your child is in a wonderful position to embrace his future with hope. There are no shackles that bind. There is no reason for pessimism. Deferred hope, which is essentially no hope, "makes the heart sick," according to God's Word (see Prov. 13:12). It stands to reason, then, that hope is part of what makes a heart whole and joyful.

The best way I know to help your child experience genuine happiness and be optimistic about his future is to teach him how to forgive and place a high value on forgiving others.

Chapter 12

SIMPLE TRUTH

Lesson #9: Sometimes You Will Lose

As much as we may try to avoid competition in our lives, we find ourselves in competitive situations. Sometimes we lose. Nobody wins *all* of the time, for *all* of life.

One of the most important lessons you will ever teach your child is how to lose and yet retain his dignity.

This doesn't mean, of course, that we should try to set our children up for failure. I have met a few parents who did just that, thinking that "failing builds character." It doesn't. What builds character is knowing how to survive the failure and turn it into a strength.

Schools place an emphasis on winning. In the wake are scores of students thrashing about in failure. Most schools either try to remediate failure by segregating failing students into special classes (which heightens the sense of failure more than alleviates it) or they punish failure. Few teachers openly address the fact that not everybody gets a top score or comes in first. That's where you come in.

Main Types of Loss

Children experience a number of losses in their lives. They lose teeth, toys, friends, races in the park, games, and their balance. Losses tend to cluster into five categories.

1. Things. Children lose items, sometimes without even knowing it.

2. Competitions. Children lose contests, and they also lose in the race for the "almighty A."

3. People and pets. Sometimes children lose parents or other loved ones to death, divorce, or abandonment. Pets run away or die. Boyfriends or girlfriends move on to other loves.

4. Face. The Oriental concept of *losing face* doesn't have a true counterpart in our culture, but the feelings associated with embarrassment come close. Losing face implies a loss of reputation, status, power, or fame.

5. Invincibility. Children think they can do anything and everything, and many in the elementary grades think they know everything. It comes as a shock to realize they don't. Each of these types of losses is a natural and normal part of childhood, within ranges. Too much loss in any one area, or a loss that is coupled with violence or abuse, can be devastating to a child.

The goal of a parent is to help a child in two ways:

- Provide skills for minimizing the severity of losses the child experiences.
- Provide skills for getting up and getting over the loss.

Minimizing and Reducing Loss

Here are twelve practical things a parent can do to help a child minimize his feeling of loss.

1. Help your child stay organized. Make sure your child has the appropriate closet and drawer space to sort out his things and maintain some sense of order.

2. Label your child's clothing and gear. Small name tags

can be stitched easily into sweaters and jackets. Your child's name can be written with indelible marker into sneakers and caps.

3. Help your child take his own mental inventory. Rather than nag your child to "not forget," ask, "Isn't there something else you need to remember to take?" Make your child do the mental exercise of sorting through his things and recalling the missing element.

4. Slow down a little. Many times children lose things because they simply are forced to hurry beyond their pace.

5. Help your child stay organized while you're on the move. When you take trips, help your child make a list of the things he is taking. Tape it to the inside of his suitcase. At each stop, let your child run through the list to make sure he has all his things. If you are moving, help your child make his own inventory of his room, and then check off the list as he unpacks in a new location.

6. Don't push your child to compete beyond his physical or mental ability. Children often enjoy a challenge, but the best challenge is only one degree beyond what the child has done in the past, not ten degrees!

7. Teach your child to love people and pets fully while they're alive. A child, and adults, too, find it easier to let go of departed friends if they know they have loved them the best they knew how. It's one thing to suffer loss and another to feel regret.

8. Teach your child how to fall—literally. Teach your young child how to "fall into a fall" and "roll with the punch." He'll hurt himself far less because he'll be better able to manipulate the direction in which he moves and he'll also provide less resistance to the surface he's about to hit. A trampoline is great for helping your child learn how to fall.

9. Provide your child activities in which balance and coordination are required, including social balance and grace. You may want to enroll your child in a ballet or gymnastics class.

Consider a "poise" class for your child—a short course that emphasizes manners, posture, and polite behaviors.

10. Help your child develop a sense of humor about himself. A child who can laugh at her own foibles is less affected by embarrassing moments.

11. Protect your child from images of violence, lewdness, and occult practices. Don't take your child to movies or let your child watch programs that depict any form of behavior you don't want your child to experience in life. Good parents don't want their children to grow up to commit murder or be murdered, be in an adulterous relationship, experience a deadly disease as the result of illicit sexual behavior, have a baby out of wedlock, or experience violence and abuse. And yet, thousands of acts a year depicting just these behaviors are fed to children on television. The television in your home should be subject to your control, not your child's.

Many programs include occult practices and practices common to Eastern religions—including the presence of shamans and spirit guides, demons, evil symbols, witchcraft tools, and the casting of spells. Your child simply doesn't need to know these things. They do not make him smarter about his culture. They teach him, in many cases, about a culture that is very different from the one of his home and neighborhood and about a culture that is different from the one his parents truly want him to have.

12. Be there as a backup for your child. He may not even need to know that you're there at times. At other times he may take great comfort in knowing you're available if something should go wrong.

Helping Your Child in Loss

There's a saying, "When you find yourself knocked down on the floor, look around to see what you might pick up while you're there." And another, "If you get run out of town, try to get to the head of the line so it looks like you're leading a parade." In other words, it's not the fact that you lose but how you recover that counts.

When your child does suffer a loss, here are ten things you can do to help him recover quickly:

1. Don't minimize the feelings that your child has about a loss. Remember, your child's feelings are valid and need expression. If your child is angry, show him how to channel that anger into a productive expenditure of energy—for example, how to go swing at baseballs in a batting cage rather than punch people. If your child is sad, let him cry or be alone for a while. Don't press your child immediately to socialize or to pretend that nothing has happened.

2. Pray with your child about the loss. Ask the Lord on your child's behalf to comfort his heart and to provide what your child needs. Encourage him to ask God for very specific provision, perhaps a new friend, another puppy, another chance, the ability to forget, or a healing of a skinned knee.

3. Encourage your child to take fairly immediate action toward replacing the loss. The child who falls off a horse is nearly always encouraged to get back on that horse as soon as possible. The same is true for other losses or falls. Allow your child a brief mourning period, and then encourage her to become a player again—to start saving for the replacement item, to go out and make new friends and to try again.

4. Teach your child how to congratulate the winner. If your child loses a contest or competition, teach him to go to the winner and with a handshake or pat on the back, say, "Congratulations." Your child doesn't need to say anything more than that word. Don't insist that she say, "You deserved to win" or "I'm glad you won." Chances are that isn't the way your child feels. If your child is genuinely happy for the other person, he might say, "I'm happy for you." Congratulating the winner with a generous smile keeps your child from becoming bitter or developing ill feelings toward a person.

5. Talk to your child about the loss. If the loss is the result of his own carelessness, your child probably knows the mistake he made. But if he says repeatedly, "I don't know why this happened," explain how you see the situation. You may be wise to wait before you have this conversation—heaping immediate criticism upon a loss only increases the pain of the moment.

In some cases, such as the death of a parent or the divorce of parents, there may be no good answers to the question of why. Let your child know that you empathize with his pain and that there are some things in this life for which we have no answers. We can know the Lord, however. He is the One who does know the answers. We can ask Him to reveal to us what we need to know in order that we can go forward in our lives with strength and stability.

Let your child know that the best lessons related to a loss do not involve knowing why something happened but in learning what happened. The why of a loss may never have an answer, but "What now?" nearly always does.

6. Map out a recovery plan with your child. Ask, "What do you think you should do now?" Direct your child's attention toward recovery. Ask if there's something she hopes you'll do to help her through this difficult time. She may say, "I need a little space to sort this out" or "Let's not bring up that person's name for a while" or "Please don't tell a certain person this happened." As much as possible, do what your child asks.

Talk about specifics as you make a plan of action. The best thing your child might do is walk tall into the schoolhouse the next day and if anybody says anything about the circumstance, respond with a smile and no words.

Give your child a handle on how to respond to teasing or ridicule. Generally speaking, looking a critic in the eye and saying nothing are far more potent than arguing or running away.

7. *Applaud your child's courage.* Let your child know that you believe she is not only going to survive this loss but emerge stronger than ever. As you see your child beginning to make attempts at regaining what has been lost or in recovering from an embarrassment, applaud your child's bravery. Let your child know that you are available to support her in any way possible.

8. *Encourage your child to reach out to other children who lose.* Very often the greatest therapy for getting over a loss is to reach out to another child who is suffering from a similar loss. Let them support each other. As your child gives comfort to someone else, she will be comforted.

9. *Teach your child to avoid using the word* never. After children have suffered a loss, they often say, "I'm never going to do that again," or "I'm never going to let that happen to me in the future." Never is a long time. Encourage your child to adjust his time frame into something reasonable. Injuries of all types have an ideal recovery time—emotional and psychological injuries included. If your child says, "I'm never going to trust anybody again," encourage him to add a time frame, such as "at least until tomorrow." Or if your child says, "I'm never going to have another boyfriend," insist that she add, "until next month." Such statements define periods of mourning for your child, after which he needs to feel no guilt for breaking a "never" vow.

10. *Do your best to find an area in which your child enjoys success.* Children can accommodate many losses if they know there is one thing in which they excel. Point out your child's strengths to him. This is especially important in a time of loss. Remind your child that there have been other times in which he was the winner or in which he excelled.

When to Fight Back?

Retaliation is only one step away from full-blown revenge. Don't let your child harbor a spirit of revenge. Teach your child early this verse of Scripture: " 'Vengeance is Mine, I will repay,' says the Lord" (Rom. 12:19).

If something of your child's has been stolen—whether a bicycle or virginity, self-esteem or a sweater—channel your child's efforts toward legal recourse. Let adults fight your child's battle in ways that are moral and just. Do your best to see that your child is justified fully. If the crime against your child has been a public one, then the reinstatement of your child to a position of honor should also be public.

If your child has been abused by someone, take action. Don't remain silent, thinking that if you ignore it your child will forget. Children do not forget abuse. They simply stuff it deep within their psyches, where it festers and smolders for years. When it erupts, the pain is devastating, often resulting in more violence and abuse. Get your child good counseling. Assure your child of your love and support. Break all association with the abuser—and take legal action. Only in these tangible ways can your child see that you are truly supportive.

School personnel have become much better informed in recent years about the nature of abuse and its symptoms. Teachers are more sensitive, as a whole, to abuse than they ever have been. But don't count on your child's teacher to be the first person to spot abuse. You have that responsibility as a parent. If your child has been molested sexually, beaten physically, or repeatedly abused verbally, even if the incident was years ago, you may want to talk to your child's teacher about the incident and what action you took as a parent to try to help your child heal. This may encourage the teacher to show a little more patience if she sees your child acting out in certain ways or in expressing unusual behaviors.

Compromise as a Response to Loss

In some cases, the best way to respond to a loss is to seek conflict resolution, which may involve mediation by a neutral party.

Rather than fight with enemies, encourage your child to look for ways in which your child and his enemy might coexist.

Introduce your child to the concept of "win-win." Very often, if one takes a giant step backward to gain greater objectivity, one can find a way in which both persons can win equally. Two small trophies are better than one. People can share an honor—one person can be class monitor for one week and another the next, alternating positions through a semester.

"Win-win" situations are only possible, however, in cases where both parties agree. And agreement can rarely be reached unless both parties are willing to talk to each other first. Encourage your child to make the first move toward someone who appears to be an enemy.

Don't allow your child to taunt others, strike out at others, threaten others, or issue challenges. In other words, don't let your child pick fights with other children. This only sets up a pattern for your child to see fighting and threatening as suitable means for getting what he wants, and the result over time is manipulative behavior.

Just as you want to preserve your child's dignity in the wake of a loss, you should encourage your child to uphold the dignity of others.

Retaining Dignity, Self-Respect, and Love

Losses chip away at our self-concept. Just as recovery from loss is important so is retaining your child's self-concept of being valuable.

Retaining dignity. A loss is a blow to a person's sense of dignity. Assure your child that a loss doesn't in any way diminish how much you value your child. This is especially important in times of divorce.

Retaining self-respect. A loss can also be a blow to a child's self-respect. You can help your child avoid this by refusing to allow her to generalize the loss. Children often say, "I'm just a dummy," or "I can't do anything." Politely, gently, but firmly point out to your child that such statements are lies and you don't like to hear your child lie about himself. If you hear such statements and let them go unchallenged, your child is going to assume by your silence that you agree with him.

I once had a student come to me with the conclusion, "I guess I'm just not college material."

"What has caused you to conclude that?" I asked.

"The D I got on the last test," he said.

"Big leap," I said. "Let's talk a little about the test. On previous exams you scored much higher. Was there something in particular that was different about this last test?"

"I didn't study as hard," he said.

"Was there a particular reason?"

"I guess I thought I already knew the material. I also had a couple of other big tests."

"And how are you doing in your other classes?" I asked.

"Pretty good. B's mostly."

"Then I'd say you're definitely college material. Stand back and look at the big picture."

He did. He told me several months later that before he had come to talk to me, he had already been to the registrar's office to see what might be involved in dropping out of the semester and transferring to a junior college elsewhere.

Don't let your child make major decisions based on minor facts or one-time events. Major decisions in life should only be based upon two long-range views, one in the direction of the past with an eye toward trends and the other toward the future with an eye toward goals. When the trends link to the goals, the decision is much more likely to be beneficial.

Retaining love. A loss can challenge a child's perception of himself as being lovable. Always assure your child that you love him in spite of the loss he has experienced. You may not *like* the fact that your child left his sweater hanging on a fence post at school. But let him know you love him just the same.

Modeling a Response to Loss

Finally, as a parent, keep in mind that your child will be copying your responses to the losses you experience in your own life. Be generous in cheering the victors. Don't harbor hatred. Don't allow yourself to be shackled by past losses but, rather, after a period of mourning, move forward in your life. If you exhibit these behaviors, your child will learn from them and also be more inclined to pay attention to what you say to him when he suffers his own losses.

Chapter 13

SIMPLE TRUTH

Lesson #10: You Always Have a Choice

Taxes, death, and a decision about how one is going to live in relationship with God are three of life's givens. There are very few other things that all people must do.

As adults, we know that. But put yourself in your child's shoes for a few minutes. By some estimates, more than ninety percent of what a child hears prior to the age of four is in the command mode: Do this. Do that. Don't touch that. Go put on your shoes. Leave your brother alone. Stop that. Children live in a tightly defined world.

The same goes for school. Teachers give mostly commands: Read this. Answer that. Write a paper. Give a speech. Memorize how to spell these words. Take a test. Sit down and be quiet. Pay attention. Do it this way.

From a child's perspective, life has very few options. Is it any wonder that teens sometimes go berserk when they leave home at eighteen? Suddenly the whole world seems full of options. A teen who has been kept tightly reined with very little opportunity to make choices frequently gets giddy with a newfound power.

As a parent you have the bulk of the responsibility for preparing your child to make wise choices. School will do only part of the job of preparing your child to weigh options and exercise sound judgment.

Taking the Lid Off the Box

Don't let your child get away with saying, "You never let me do anything," or "You never trust me." In all likelihood, you have let your child do a great many things on his own. If not, however, then take notice. You *need* to take the lid off the box in which you are attempting to keep your child safe from life. Your child needs to have experience making choices, even if some of them aren't perfect.

Recognizing options. Help your child recognize options. Too often, children have tunnel vision. The main reason is they simply don't know other choices exist! It's difficult to imagine a different way of life if you have no one to paint a picture of it for you.

If your teen feels stuck in a dead end, sit down with him and make a list of other possibilities. This is especially important as your child nears the end of high school. Talk candidly with your child about all the choices available to him. College may not be the best choice. That's difficult for many parents to accept these days because in our society the majority of high school graduates go on to college, even if for just a semester! Fifty years ago, less than ten percent of the adult workforce had college degrees.

Your child should consider the options of vocational training, military service, or working, even if she seems to be college-bound. In researching alternatives, she'll be much happier with the final decision she makes. As she applies to college, make sure she applies to several—at least *two* of which are certain to accept her. That way, your child will still retain the privilege to choose where she goes to study.

Don't place too much emphasis on a particular college.

In the long run, your child's ability to make a choice about college is much more important than a college's prerogative to choose her.

Prioritizing and ranking. As your child lists options, encourage him to weigh each one carefully and then to rank the options. Each option will no doubt have certain advantages and disadvantages. Eventually your child will need to conclude that some choices are better *for him* than others.

Sequencing. As your child lists choices, help him see that choices tend to be bridged to other choices. Children can understand this concept easily if you direct their attention to a tree. If a person follows one branch and then follows various other limbs and eventually twigs, the person will find himself at a very different part of the tree from where he'd be otherwise. In like manner, choices made today set a trend that will affect tomorrow.

Unfortunately, we often don't know whether we are making big decisions or little ones. We are forced simply to make the *next* decision. Still, we must do our best to see that decision in its broader context.

Help your child see beyond the moment. Young children don't have a concept of passing days. They take time moment by moment. Older children, however, do have a capacity to think ahead. Talk to your child about "one day" and "some day." Help your child anticipate the day when he leaves home and is on his own.

Schools, by and large, do a poor job of this. A child enters third grade and studies the material put in front of him. He goes on to fourth grade and studies the material of that grade. A fourth grade teacher may draw a correlation back to third grade, but that is usually in a review session. Rarely does a teacher stop to say, "Can you see how important it was for you to learn how to read so that you could study history now?" In like manner, the fourth grade teacher probably does little to help a child see how what he is studying will prepare him for ninth grade or twelfth grade. Children in school often have what I call "future blindness." They rarely are given glimpses into how material is going to be applied in coming years.

In life, however, sequential expectations abound. A person learns to walk before he runs. In giving your child glimpses into the future, you will not only motivate him to get more out of the present body of knowledge but also tell him to be ready for the future when it arrives.

Making a choice. It's not enough to help your child list options or see them in terms of appropriateness or future impact. You must also insist that your child ultimately *make* a choice.

You can help your child do this by giving him choices that relate to very specific things in his life. "Do you want to wear the blue dress or the yellow one?" "Do you want carrots or peas as your vegetable?"

At the outset, give your young child only two choices. As he grows, expand the list of options. Don't let your child cop out by saying, "You decide." Insist that your child make the decision in a timely manner. Standing all day in front of the counter isn't good decision making. Neither is making rash choices. Give your child a few minutes to think through an option and then call for a response.

Holding an Opinion, Having a Conviction

Part of your child's choices involves convictions.

Years ago, I had several debate team members in one of my speech classes. I asked one young man toward the end of the season, "Now that you've debated both sides of this issue on several occasions, what is *your* opinion?"

He said, "Which position do you want me to take, pro or con?"

"Neither," I said. "I want to know what you personally have decided. You've gathered an entire file drawer full of arguments and evidence. Which set of facts has influenced you personally? What do *you* think?"

He stared at me blankly. "Which side do you want to hear about?" he asked again.

"Don't you have an opinion?" I asked.

He said, "I've been trained not to have an opinion and not to be emotionally involved in the issue. If you're emotionally involved, then you can't debate as clearly. Your feelings get in the way."

That might be good debate-coach advice during a debate season, but it's a lousy way to approach life. The end result is a concern only with expediency. The truth and a sense of personal conviction are quickly lost in the shuffle and quickly can be deemed unimportant.

Teach your child that it is entirely appropriate for him to hold some opinions that are deeply embedded in beliefs and values. Otherwise your child is likely to face choices as a computer might, without any concern for knowledge that is gained intuitively.

Let your child know about your own deep convictions—about the beliefs that you consider to be inviolable bedrock.

Three Main Areas of Choice

There are three main choices your child needs to begin to make for himself at very early ages. These are all matters subject to the will and are decisions that even fairly young children can make.

1. Choose how to respond. An earlier chapter discussed how a child can *choose* to be happy or sad. Attitudes are subject to the will. A person can choose to alter behavior and feelings after an initial instinctual response, just as he can choose to change his mind when presented new information.

One of the things my mother told me often when I was a child was this: "Nobody has control over how you feel but you." Don't let your child grow up believing that others are in control of his feelings.

Many children and adults say to others, "You made me feel this way." A person may have done something to your child, even something very wrong, but the response to another person's action is subject to your child's will.

Your child also has the prerogative to hold his own dreams. Others may influence him to hold prejudices, but ultimately your child must face the fact that he hates because he chooses to hate. Others may influence your child to hold certain opinions or beliefs, but your child must be taught that he is ultimately responsible for his own values, including certain beliefs about God and Jesus Christ.

In my opinion, no child should be allowed to lay blame for his boredom on someone else. Children often moan, "This is boring." The implication is that somebody else made it boring, or that it is boring of its own regard. Boredom is an attitude over which your child has total control. Encourage your child to find something of interest in the situation and, if he cannot, to retreat into the world of his own imagination, where things should never be boring.

2. *Choose what to think about.* Your child's thoughts are his exclusive property. Teach your child early that nobody should be allowed to invade the realm of his imagination without his permission and that nobody can take away any knowledge that your child plants in his own mind. What your child learns is his to keep.

If your child suffers from nightmares, especially violent and recurring ones, take that as a sign that in some way your child has not been saying no to certain messages. Find out what is sparking her imagination and remove that stimulus from her life.

Teach your teen that wrong behavior begins in the imagination. If your child can control the thoughts in his mind, he will have a much easier time controlling the impulses in his body.

3. Choose to say no to evil and yes to good. Let your child know that he has the privilege of saying no to things that are evil and to embrace what is good.

If your child doesn't want to be in a situation he finds scary, he should be allowed to leave. Don't insist that your child stay in a dark place if it frightens him. Don't require your young child to go into a so-called "fun house." Most children are very sensitive to atmospheres that are marked by confusion or permeated with undercurrents of hate, rebellion, or trickery. If your child has an averse reaction to a scene in a movie, even something you consider innocent fantasy, walk out of the theater. Don't require your child to take into her spirit something that she intuitively feels is bad.

Especially give your child permission to say no to:

Verbal abuse. I recently heard a four-year-old boy say to an older child in a park, "My mother told me that I don't have to listen to you calling me those names." He immediately covered his ears with his hands and walked away. Smart mother, smart son.

Physical abuse. One of the bravest and smartest children I've ever known was Eddie. He was short and skinny, and as you might imagine, a favorite target for taller and more robust boys. One day I heard an older and larger boy tell Eddie that he was going to knock his block off. Eddie stood his ground, stared right back at the bigger child and said, "I give you permission to do that."

"What do you mean, you give me permission?" the mean-spirited child taunted.

"You might think you are hitting me, but if you hit me, it's because I'm letting you hit me," Eddie said.

The bigger child was so flustered by this comment that

he mumbled, "You're not worth skinning my knuckles," and walked off. Eddie not only didn't get hit, but he actually gained some playground power that day.

Sexual abuse. Teach your child early which parts of his body are private. Let him know that if anyone attempts to touch him in a way that he thinks is wrong, he should be bold in saying, "I don't want you to do that" and that he should run away from the person as quickly as possible and tell a teacher or other adult what has happened.

Let your child know that you are her ally and that if anyone abuses her verbally, physically, or sexually, you will step in. Assure your child that no matter what another person may threaten, you want to know the truth and that together the two of you can then decide what to do. (Abusers frequently threaten children that something bad will happen to them or to someone they love if they tell. Alert your child in advance that this is a trick that abusers use in order to get their way and that you want your child to be smart enough not to fall for it. She should come and tell you immediately.) Then believe your child if she comes to you with a story of abuse. Applaud your child for attempting to run from evil.

Choose to act first. The self-starters in life are generally those who succeed. Show your child ways in which he might initiate a conversation or be the first to do a kind deed. Praise your child for taking positive, proactive steps. The child who sits back and waits for life to come his way abdicates his right to choose.

Don't Fall Victim to Pressure

Several years ago, two young women came to my office within a matter of hours. They reflected vastly different capacities to make sound choices.

Tina came first. Scott, her old high school boyfriend, had

called and asked her to marry him. Tina didn't have a clue as to how to answer him.

"Tell me about Scott and about your relationship," I said. She proceeded to give me a glowing report. Scott certainly sounded like a knight in shining armor.

"What's the down side?" I asked. "What's wrong with Scott or with your choosing to marry Scott?"

"Well," she said with some hesitation, "he wants to get married right away and live right there in our old hometown. That means that I would have a much harder time finishing college. It also means that I might not get to do a little traveling, which I've always wanted to do. That doesn't matter to Scott, but it does matter to me."

"Do you feel as if you'd be short-changed in some way if you married Scott right now?" I asked.

"Yes," she admitted. "I looked forward to college all through high school, and if I marry Scott now at the end of my sophomore year, I'm going to miss out on half of the fun I thought I'd have in college. On the other hand, if I don't marry Scott, I might never have another chance to get married . . . or at least to marry someone with as many good qualities as Scott. I haven't met anybody yet here at school that is as attractive to me as Scott."

"How many guys do you think might exist on the earth who would be good husbands for you?" I asked.

She stared back at me without an answer. "You must have some ball-park figure," I said.

"I guess I've always thought in terms of a one-and-only," she said. "But I guess there are probably lots of guys who would make good husbands for me."

We talked for two hours, and during that time I discovered that Tina had had a difficult time breaking up with Scott in high school, that she hadn't really wanted to date him steadily in the first place but no one else had asked her out, and that she didn't really have a strong desire to return to her hometown to live—at least not for a few years.

I sensed that Tina was feeling pressured to make a decision she wasn't ready to make, so I asked, "What would Scott do if you told him you'd have an answer for him by the time you return home this summer (which was still about three months away)?"

"I think he would take that as a no," she said. "He wants an answer right away."

"You really don't think he could wait ninety days for an answer that might impact the rest of both of your lives?" I asked.

"You're right," she said. "I'm just too pressured." She had finally made a decision. Scott would have to wait for an answer, and if he couldn't wait, that would be a sign to her that he wasn't really the one for her.

Two hours later Becky walked into my office. "I just wanted you to know that Don asked me to marry him last night and I said 'yes.'"

"Congratulations," I said. "Are you both really sure about this?"

"Really sure," she said. "I've dated about ten guys since I first started dating in high school, and it's just as Mom always told me, you know when you meet the right one. Don has faults and problems, but he's right for me, and he puts up with my faults and problems pretty well, too."

"How long have you two been dating?" I asked.

"Six months," she said. "But don't worry; we aren't rushing into this. We've both still got two years of college to finish, and we talked it over. We decided it would be a much smarter idea to wait until we are both finished with school and have jobs. We've set our wedding date for the Christmas after we graduate."

"Do you think you can wait that long?" I teased.

"We'll just have to," she said with a smile. "We talked about that and decided it was a matter of pacing."

These two young women obviously had different relationships with their young men and different criteria related to their marriage choices, but one thing was clear: Tina was feeling pressured to make a major decision without having adequate time to think through her decision. The pressure was keeping her from recognizing all her options. Becky was feeling no pressure. She and Don had made some sound decisions that showed an ability to weigh various options and choose among them. Their passion was in no way diminished by their rational approach to decisionmaking, including a weighing of priorities and sequencing.

As I got better acquainted with Tina and Becky over the next two years, I learned far more about their childhoods. Tina had very strong-willed, controlling parents who gave her few and only minor choices to make in her life. Becky, on the other hand, had parents who had taught her that life was full of choices and that it was her privilege to choose the best that life had to offer to her. When it came time for these young women to choose their mates for life, they had very different capabilities, primarily because they had very different levels of experience in making choices.

Never pressure your child unduly to make a choice about which your child is uncomfortable. At the same time, find out why your child is uncomfortable about it. What is he scared will happen if he makes a choice? It could be he is unable to visualize consequences or isn't aware that even after he makes a bad choice he is able to modify it later.

Living with the Consequences

There's a difference in insisting that your child stick by certain choices and forcing your child to live in misery because he has made a bad choice. You need to talk candidly about two terms, commitment and vows.

Commitment. If another person is involved in a choice and has committed himself to a decision (including perhaps time and resources), then your child has an obligation to fulfill that commitment or repay all the other person has lost.

Teach your child this lesson early. If your child and another child, for example, decide to open a lemonade stand together and they go fifty-fifty into the venture and then your child decides he'd rather go to the swimming pool instead, he needs to face the fact that he has made a *commitment* to the other child. He either needs to keep that commitment or be prepared to give full ownership of all the equipment as well as any proceeds to the other child. Plus, he should apologize to the child for bailing out.

Don't let your child walk away from commitments without fulfilling them in a way that is fair to the party left holding the bag.

Vows. Vows are nearly always made evoking God's help. If your child asks God's help in doing something, then she needs to stick with the vow she has made. She is free only if she has full assurance from others who witnessed the vow that God has released her from it.

Discourage your child from making vows lightly. They are extremely serious matters—earthly verbal contracts bearing the full weight of God's heavenly law.

Guilt and bad choices. In many cases, a child will feel guilty over making a bad choice and stay in a bad situation simply because of that guilt—or because he feels he must prove to his parents that the choice wasn't all that bad. Give your child permission to repent of bad choices and to make new, better choices. Again, proper restitution may be required.

Keep in mind that commitment, vows, and guilt are terms

that schoolteachers rarely weave into class discussion. What your child learns about the nature of commitment and vows she will learn primarily from watching you relate to others. Do you fulfill your contractual responsibilities? Do you keep your vows? Do you refuse to be easily swayed by temporary circumstances that might force a less resilient person to abandon certain choices?

Modeling Good Choices

Your child watches very closely the choices you make and the way you make them—whether it's picking out a ripe cantaloupe at the supermarket or deciding who in your department will get the promotion.

As you make choices . . .

1. Let your child see you taking time to make rational, thoughtful choices. Let him see you weighing the options presented by the insurance agent, reading reference materials that compare options, or talking over choices with your spouse and other trusted advisors.

2. Let your child overhear you praying about certain choices, asking for God's wisdom and direction.

3. Talk to your child about the decisions you make. Let her know your reasons and what processes you went through before reaching a decision. Consult your teenager on some of the choices you are facing. Get her input. Talk over with her all of the concerns you might have and how you are going about gathering information that may impact your final decision.

4. Talk to your child about the decisions he is facing. Listen intently to how your child is weighing information and for clues as to whom might be influencing his decisions.

Make certain that your choices . . .

- are based on sound evidence.

- reflect a concern for the benefit of all who are involved, including your child.
- are part of a greater pattern of decisions and values in your life.
- are not lip service but taken seriously.
- are the ones you believe are pleasing to the heavenly Father and have potential for good both now and for eternity.

If you model this brand of making choices to your child, he will be well equipped to make responsible choices, no matter what the circumstance he is facing.

Chapter 14

SIMPLE TRUTH
Lesson #11: Seek Truth and Speak Truthfully

I do not think I have ever been as upset about a student's behavior as I was about Mitch's.

Mitch was one of the most talented public speaking students I have ever had in a lower division class. In delivery and content his presentations were superb. He was also one of the laziest students I have ever had. Mitch did only the bare minimum to get an A. He, of course, thought he was clever and even said on one occasion, "Why do more than you have to to win?"

The stipulations in this particular course were clearly set out the first day of class. The formula was precise—each assignment, quiz, exam, and final exam was allocated a certain number of points, and grades were figured against a straight percentage scale. Since grading speeches is a fairly subjective exercise, I usually required the students to grade each speech given. Half of a student's grade on any given speech was the average score of all the numerical grades submitted by his peers. In short, grading for the class was well announced and as objective as possible. Mitch played the points well. Going into the final exam, he had earned *exactly* ninety percent of the total points, the lowest allowable percentage for an A.

The final exam was not one of my own design but one created by the entire department. As in most colleges, Speech

101 was a required course, so sections of it were taught each semester by different teachers and graduate teaching assistants. The one uniform element to the course, apart from the text and general syllabus, was the final exam.

Mitch clearly heard the rules regarding the final exam: "Don't mark on the test sheet; mark only on the answer sheet." This rule also was stated boldly at the top of both the test and answer sheets. Students were asked to put their social security numbers on both sheets, however, as a means of test control. As students completed their final exams, they put answers in one pile, test sheets in another. Except for Mitch. He turned in only an answer sheet.

I knew within seconds after the exam period what had happened. And I knew the implications. The Speech 101 final exam for that semester had been compromised.

It was a well-known fact among students and professors at this particular university that fraternity and sorority members were frequently assigned to steal exams and put copies of them in a secure "house file" for review by other house members. Good students were expected to contribute their knowledge in this way to their fraternity brothers and sorority sisters.

I mentally calculated about how long I thought it would take Mitch to walk to his fraternity and back, with a quick stop at a duplicating machine en route. I expected to see Mitch again within an hour and fifteen minutes, so I proceeded to grade the exams while I waited in my office for him. I also alerted the course coordinator that I felt certain the exam had been compromised and that other sections should perhaps be given an alternate test form.

In grading the exams, I was surprised to find that Mitch had _not_ been smart enough to transfer all his marks from the test to his answer sheet. Only about forty percent of the answer sheet had been filled in and, of those answers, he had missed four questions—his usual ninety percent. But this time the correct answers amounted to only thirty-six percent of the total exam. Such a low final exam score brought his total grade for the course to a B.

In precisely one hour and ten minutes, Mitch came rushing into my office, in tears no less. He couldn't have been sorrier for what he had done. He had opened his notebook in his next class and discovered the test there. He couldn't understand how he could have been so careless. His excuse was a masterful piece of drama.

I agreed with Mitch. "I also don't understand how you could have been so careless, Mitch. If you were going to take the exam from the classroom, you should at least have been careful to transfer all your answers to the answer sheet. And, if you had at least half a class period to stare at the exam, you could have erased the answers that you wrote directly on the test sheet."

Mitch blanched. He hadn't realized that he had failed to transfer all the answers. Forgetting to erase the answers on the test sheet was an obvious goof.

I asked him what class he had just been in. I figured that if he was, in fact, telling me the truth that I could verify his excuse. Mitch didn't have an answer but started to backpedal. "Did I say I was in a class?" he said. "I was in the library."

I didn't say anything. "You aren't going to hold this against me, are you?" he pleaded. "Like, lower my grade or anything?"

"Well, actually," I said as calmly as possible, "the numbers pretty much speak for themselves, Mitch. The thirty-six you scored on the exam gives you a total that results in a percentage of eighty-four."

"You can't give me a B," he bellowed. "I'm an A student."

"How do you figure that?" I asked.

And then the threats started. If I gave Mitch a B in Speech 101, he would be dropped from a certain competitive club on the campus, and if that happened he was likely to have his scholarship taken away, and if that happened his father would likely withdraw the fairly major gift he was preparing to bestow upon the university. He was now in the midst of a full-blown tantrum.

I couldn't resist responding, "Lame excuses, Mitch? Threats? Tantrums? Is this the way you live your life?" He stormed from my office.

I sensed the issue wasn't resolved fully and, sure enough, that afternoon there was a flurry of phone calls. Eventually, the grade I gave Mitch was overturned; he was given an A for the course by the department head. The club, however, to which he belonged was dissolved a few years later for blatant intercollegiate cheating. Mitch had plans of going on to law school and becoming an attorney. I don't know if he did, but it's a scary thought.

That five-hour episode with Mitch told me a lot about his upbringing. Mitch had been taught that expediency was more valuable than truth and that power was preferable to character.

Those are dangerous lessons to teach a child. But if a child comes to school having learned them, there is very little a school system can do to change that child's value system. Such a student invariably finds a loophole because he's always looking for one.

Children who believe that expediency is more valuable than truth find a paper to copy or ask a friend to do their homework in exchange for another favor. They manipulate others to do their bidding and make them look good in class. They ultimately have little interest in learning content but a great deal in power struggles with their peers and teachers. Theirs is a quest for authority, not knowledge.

A Root of Deception

On the surface one might say, "Mitch stole an exam." But his fault was not so much stealing as it was believing a string of lies and then acting on them. Those lies included:

- You need to steal this exam (for the good of the whole).
- You are the best person to steal this exam (because you are such a smart guy).
- You can get away with this if you are clever.
- You can con your teacher.
- If you can't con your teacher, you can con somebody else into believing you're innocent.
- You don't have to play by the rules that apply to other students (because you're special).
- The school is here to do you a favor.
- Grades count because of what they get you, not because they reflect what you know.
- Getting what you want is the only thing that matters.
- You can buy or bully your way into what you don't earn.

These sound like lines taken straight from a conversation in the Garden of Eden. Sadly, the school itself underscored the practicality of these lies to Mitch.

As far as I am concerned, lies are at the root of virtually everything we call sin and misbehavior. They are the verbalization of pride.

A school will do little to warn your child against the dangers of pride. Indeed, schools often call pride good—something firmly rooted in team morale or individual achievement. Children are taught in schools to be proud of who they are and what they have accomplished. Granted, this is a limited definition of pride. But it is important to recognize that schools hardly ever criticize a person for having too much self-esteem.

A Working Definition of Truthfulness

What is truth?

Philosophers have debated that question for millennia. The Bible teaches these things are true:

God is creator and source. He is the absolute and almighty king of the universe, of all that is seen and unseen. As the sovereign Lord, He is all-knowing, all-powerful, all-loving, and eternal. He is the beginning and the end, the great I AM.

We are created. We have a beginning in time. We are subject to God's plan and its wise and just execution and we are the beneficiaries of His great love.

God desires to be in relationship with us. He loves us and longs to have fellowship with us. He leaves the choice of a response to us. If we choose not to have that relationship, we are separated from God and suffer the consequences inherent in separation. If we choose to have that relationship, He gives us the fullness of Himself. In choosing a relationship with God, we also must choose to live by the rules He has established for our good.

The person who attempts to deny God's existence and live according to his own rules has bought into the deception of all deceptions: "Surely God didn't mean what He has said ... surely you are an exception to His rules ... surely you won't die" (see Gen. 3:4). A person who buys into this basic set of lies easily buys into all other lies.

The great mystery, of course, is that the person who yields his life to God's authority is the one who finds most self-fulfillment!

A number of people believe God is a harsh judge, just

waiting to pounce upon them for each misdeed of their lives. God judges, to be sure, but He is just. But the one whom God judges ultimately is the enemy of our souls. His battle is not with us, but with the one who initially rebelled against Him. We are *evidence* in the courtroom drama of the ages, not defendants. We are witnesses called to testify by our actions to the Lordship of Jesus Christ or the sovereignty of Satan.

The *truth* is that God is in charge . . . we aren't. Believing otherwise puts a person into a position of rebellion against God. That rebellion nearly always manifests itself as a general rebellion against all who bear authority—including teachers and school systems.

Teaching Truth to Your Child

How can you teach truth to your child?

First and foremost, model truth—yield to those who have authority over you as a parent.

Yes, you can actively protest against laws that are contrary to God's law. But you must do so *within* God's law. Be loving and have loving intentions.

The One to whom you must ultimately yield is God Himself. Let your child hear you sincerely ask God for wisdom to train your child and make decisions to his benefit.

One of the best ways to model yielding behavior is to let your child see you consulting God's Word frequently. The Church has proclaimed for centuries that the Bible is the authoritative Word of God to us. God does not reveal truth to a person that is not verifiable in His Word, by either stated principle or recorded practice. When in doubt, go to the Bible and see what it has to say about an issue. Let your child see you consulting God's Word as the definitive, authoritative source of information on which you base your life.

Parents are also called to yield authority to police,

judges, employers, and pastors. The respect you show those who have authority over your life will be copied by your child.

You don't have to fawn over others or become a doormat. You do need to answer them respectfully and regard them with esteem.

Pray for those who have authority over your life. Let your child hear you making such petitions to God. The day you begin to ridicule authority figures is the day your child begins to rebel against authority—including your own!

Require your child to show respect for those in authority, including yourself as a parent. Insist that your child respect his other parent, even if that person is no longer living in the home. Insist that your child respect your spouse—even if that person isn't the child's natural or birth parent. Insist that your child respect his grandparents.

In very practical terms, don't allow back talk, ridicule, snide comments, mean teasing, nasty gestures, or other forms of resistance to authority. Be wary in allowing your child to use slang when referring to authority figures. Slang expressions for policemen, clergy, and national leaders can be a form of ridicule.

Don't let your child show disrespect for the institutions you consider important. In a practical way, this refers to the property and symbols of various institutions. Teach your child to show respect for the flag, those who are wearing military uniforms, and crosses.

Insist that your child show respect for those who have died and to act in a respectful manner in funeral homes, mausoleums, and cemeteries.

Never reward your child for being "clever" in bypassing authority. The child who senses that a parent approves of expediency over truth is going to seek out further means of expediency—which means even more clever lies and more subtle deceit.

Insist that your child speak truthfully. Teach your child that truthful communication is:

- *Accurate.* It is rooted in evidence that in most cases should be verifiable.
- *Honest.* It is a genuine expression of how your child sees a circumstance.
- *Whole.* Truth inevitably includes both good and bad elements. There is no truth in not telling the whole story or in omitting certain facts.

The Scriptures teach that out of the mouths of two or three witnesses the truth is established (see Deut. 17:6; 2 Cor. 13:1). Don't believe everything your child tells you at face value. If you have doubts about the veracity of his statements, subject him to the testimony of other witnesses.

Especially require your child to speak the truth about herself and her own convictions. Give your child ample opportunity to practice stating her opinions, including statements of her faith. Require your child to vocalize positive statements about herself. Help her develop a realistic and balanced opinion about her own strengths and weaknesses.

Be consistent in what you require from your child. Truth lasts. It doesn't change. It isn't situational. Furthermore, truth does not contradict any of the behaviors we associate with a person who is leading a godly life: love, joy, peace, longsuffering, kindness, goodness, faithfulness, gentleness, and self-control (see Gal. 5:22–23). We cannot conclude that a person is operating in the truth if he is mean, self-centered, adulterous, violent, heretical, envious, murderous, and so forth (see Gal. 5:19–21 for a list of behaviors that are called works of the flesh).

Truth does not coexist with lust, greed, or pride.

The truthful life is lived in obedience to God's commandments. The truthful person attempts to do and say what Jesus would do and say.

Model a truthful life to your child, and your child will seek to establish such a life of his own.

Recognizing Lies for What They Are

As you teach your child about truth, also teach your child to recognize lies when he sees them.

Point out errors of discernment and judgment. Don't let your child go unchallenged if she draws a false conclusion about something or misinterprets hard evidence. Let your child know that people will sometimes tell her lies as a means of exerting power over her.

Jill was distressed that she always seemed to be so weak in withstanding the sexual advances of the young men she dated.

"What makes you think you're weak?" I said.

"I don't know," she said. "I just give in too easily. It's like I space out and go into victim mode."

I asked her if she had been molested as a child, since this seems to be a frequent response of those who are sexually or physically abused. She said no.

"Was there someone who told you as a child that you were weak?"

"Oh, yes," she said. "I have three older brothers, and they were forever telling me I was a sissy and didn't have any guts or backbone."

"You believed them," I said, not as a question but as a conclusion.

"What do you mean?" she said.

"It seems to me that because they were older and bigger and stronger you believed at face value what they said. You came to a conclusion that you probably were just what they said you were."

"I think I did," Jill said eagerly. "But what do I do about that now?"

"Start believing a new set of facts. Start believing the truth I'm telling you today: You are not a weakling, a wimp, or a coward. You have a backbone. You have courage. You are able to withstand temptation." I had seen Jill in enough situations where she verbalized strong opinions or gave a strong testimony about her faith to know that she was a young woman of remarkable courage and conviction.

"But I really am weak, I think," she countered.

"Do you ever voice an opinion of your own?" I asked.

"Sure," she said.

"Do you ever make decisions by yourself?"

"Yes."

"Do you always go along with the crowd when they are planning to do something you know is wrong?"

"No."

"The ability to voice opinions, make decisions, and act on your own values are all signs of inner strength, Jill," I concluded. "Start believing that you can say no to lust, too."

If your child is believing lies today about himself, help him face up to them. Teach him to start believing a truth that is in line with God's Word to him.

Getting to the truth. Help your child develop criteria for determining if something is the truth. Even young children should be taught to question certain statements made by their peers.

Such questions might be:

- What is the underlying motive here? Who stands to benefit and why? Why is this being said about the person?

- Does this match up with other behavior I have witnessed personally or other things that I have heard the person say in the past?
- Do consequences bear out the validity of this statement?
- Who can confirm whether this is true?

Fighting falsehoods. At times, we are all victims of lies that others tell about us. Teach your child early in life that those who tell gossip about others tend to be jealous of one's success or are very unsure of themselves. They're hoping to build up their own reputation by pulling down that of another person.

Lovingly speak the truth. Teach your child what to do in the face of lies: to speak the truth in a loving manner. A child should feel free to state the truth about himself. He doesn't need to engage in a name-calling match or give volumes of evidence to justify his claims. He simply can say, "That isn't true. The truth is ___" and let it go at that.

In the wake of such a statement, the best option is nearly always to hold one's head high and live with integrity so that falsehood has no peg on which to hang its hat.

At times, children spread truths about another child—maliciously. In many ways, these statements are also lies because they fail to address the full character of the child or the circumstance.

A child can respond with, "That is only partly true. The truth also includes the fact that ..." and go on to say something positive.

I once witnessed a student come upon a group of her peers who just happened to be talking about her at the time. They were concluding that Lydia was a "slosh-head" because they had seen her drinking beer the previous Saturday night.

They were embarrassed when they turned to see Lydia standing nearby, obviously taking in every word.

Lydia handled the situation in a superb manner. She said, "You're right, I was drinking last Saturday night. On Sunday morning I was very sick, and I made a decision not to do that again. I hope you will help me stick by my decision." She completely defused their gossip and ended up being the object of their consolation!

If there is a truth about your child's background that might subject her to taunting or teasing, bring it up early in her life and forearm your child. The matter may relate to your child's paternity, a handicap or lack of ability, your marital status at the time of your child's birth, a matter of race or socioeconomic status, or a matter of your child's cultural or national heritage. Rehearse with your child what to say if someone attempts to hurt her with verbal abuse.

One of the best forms of recourse is to walk away and say nothing. Another recourse is to admit that what the person is saying is true and then add, "But that's only part of the truth. Here's more." Your child can then relate a statement or two about himself that is positive.

In arming your child this way, you are sending a signal to your child that truth resides in knowing the whole of a matter. Truth is never verified by partial evidence.

Lies destroy. Finally, teach your child about the deadliness of lies. Lies destroy. They kill a part of the human spirit, they tear apart relationships, and they rob us of the very things we are often trying to protect by a lie. Lies beget lies. The person who tells one lie nearly always is forced to tell another to cover it up, yet another to cover up the first two, and so forth. Ultimately an entire web of lies is spun.

Sir Walter Scott said it well: "Oh, what a tangled web we weave, when first we practice to deceive."

Point out to your child examples in which lies have

brought about downfall or pain. Your child can probably recall a few examples of his own. Ultimately, lying never brings about lasting or eternal benefit.

Association with liars. Don't let your child associate with children who habitually lie. Such peers cloud your child's ability to distinguish right from wrong. Find new friends for your child.

Knowledge vs. Truth

Keep in mind always that schools are about the business of teaching knowledge—facts, concepts, principles, rules, and procedures. They are not in the business of conveying truth.

A teacher may punish a lie just as he punishes any other form of behavior, but the punishment is nearly always meted out as a means of maintaining group norms or group decorum. A teacher does not punish in order to bring about value reform in a student.

Schools claim to be repositories of truth, but in reality they're only depositories of books, maps, charts, films, and videos. Public schools cannot, by law, proclaim truth, because truth is deeply embedded in the deepest beliefs and values held by an individual.

Churches often proclaim truth. But very few churches provide real-life practicums in which the church members must be fully accountable to each other for the truthfulness of the way they live their lives.

The realm of values and belief is the home. It is there that truth is ultimately defined.

Chapter 15

SIMPLE TRUTH
Lesson #12: Choose Carefully Whom or What You Will Worship

The haunting lyrics of an old Bob Dylan song say it well: "Everybody's got to *serve* somebody."

Built into our human nature is a desire to worship something greater than ourselves. This has been noted by both archaeologists and historians observing the earliest human cultures. It is a phenomenon recorded by anthropologists who have found it in the most remote regions of the world. We human beings have a void within us that we all seek to fill with the presence of another being.

Most of us conclude that this tendency is a built-in "God response." Whether we consciously recognize it or not, God is wooing us continually. He has created us for Himself, and there is a part of us that is never fully satisfied until we have a relationship with Him.

Schools rarely teach this to children—even many schools associated with churches. They may teach about God and say that God exists, God loves, and we must respond to God. Those are didactic lessons. A true "God response" is made spiritually and enacted by spiritual behavior. It is not a fact, concept, principle, rule, or procedure to be learned by the mind. It is something that is *done* by the *heart*.

Learning about worship and worshiping are two very

different things. Schools may teach *about* worship, but few give full opportunity for students to do so.

What Is Worship?

Worship is utter and complete adoration of God—both for what He has done and who He is. It is recognizing His majesty and glory.

While praise is marked by joyful sounds—singing, shouting, clapping, and the playing of instruments—worship is expressed by profound silence. Praise is marked by dancing and jumping, but the posture of worship is bowing—both literally and in the heart.

I once had occasion to stand on the south rim of the Grand Canyon formed by the Colorado River. Neither the person standing next to me nor I said a word. We just stood there for fifteen minutes, completely absorbed in the grandeur of that sight. Miles and minutes later while we were on the road toward Flagstaff, my traveling companion said, "There just weren't any words important enough."

It had been a moment of worship for us both. There was no way a finite vocabulary could give expression about One who had made something of such stunning magnitude and beauty.

Worship experiences are rare in most people's lives. They are nearly always recalled with a sense of longing to return. Worship is intense and transcendent. A person in worship has little regard for time and is oblivious to hunger, thirst, and other basic needs.

It is as Elijah described:

And behold, the LORD passed by, and a great and strong wind tore into the mountains and broke the rocks in pieces before the LORD, but the LORD was not in the wind; and after the wind an earthquake, but the LORD was not in the earthquake; and after the earthquake a fire, but the LORD was not in the fire; and after the fire a still small voice. So it was, when Elijah heard it, that he wrapped his face in his mantle and went out and stood in the entrance of the cave (1 Kings 19:11–13).

Worship flows from and pulls a person toward the very core of the center. No words reside there. In the awesome presence of the Almighty, no words need to be spoken. All that is needed is available.

How Can a Parent Teach Worship?

How can you teach something that is so deeply personal and bound up in experience?

1. You should teach your child to distinguish between praise, admiration, desire, and worship. These are four distinct concepts, with very different expressions.

- *Praise* relates to what God has done through our Lord Jesus Christ and to what we perceive Him to be doing in our lives. Praise responds to the fact that our sins have been forgiven and we are destined for eternal life with our heavenly Father.
- *Admiration* is what we feel toward other human beings. It is a response to what we perceive to be an expression in that person's life of the best and highest human qualities. Admiration is objective.
- *Desire* is longing to have or possess something or someone. It is highly subjective. It is often expressed in terms of love—by saying, for example, "I really love that person"—but it is also a concept deeply rooted in want.
- *Worship* is a union of our spirit with God's Spirit. It is

the Holy Spirit bearing witness with our spirits that we are children of God.

Praise and worship belong solely to God—Father, Son, and Holy Spirit.

Praise of your child is ultimately praise for what God is doing in and through your child. When you give words of praise to your child, you rarely say, "I praise you, Johnny, for what you just did." Rather, you say, "Good job, Johnny." Your expression is more accurately a statement of deep admiration and love. Underlying it, however, can also be the meaning, "Praise You, Father, for what You are doing in Johnny's life."

Stop to give some thought to how and why you praise your child. Some parents praise their children as if they're gods! These parents simply cannot bear the thought of not having their children with them always; their very identity flows from having children. When a parent feels this way, he or she inevitably gives the child anything the child wants. It is an aberrant form of sacrificial worship. They pay homage to their child, letting their child say and do pretty much what he wants. Worship of your child is dangerous—not only for you, but for your child.

The Scriptures teach us clearly that God alone is worthy of our praise and worship. Our children are ours to love. They are never to be the object of our worship.

2. *You can talk to your child about what it means to worship God and Him alone*. Share some of your own worship experiences with your child as best you can. Let your child catch a glimpse of the awesome majestic King whom you worship and serve. Let your child know that there are spiritual experiences that are too deep for words.

Also let your child know that God is a jealous God. In teaching your child the Ten Commandments, place your emphasis on the first three.

You shall have no other gods before Me. You shall not make for yourself a carved image—any likeness of anything that is in heaven above, or that is in the earth beneath, or that is in the water under the earth; you shall not bow down to them nor serve them. . . . You shall not take the name of the LORD your God in vain (Ex. 20:3–7).

We are required to worship God, but it is also our highest privilege.

Let your child know that even beyond his love and respect for you, he is to love, respect, and *worship* God. Willingly yield that highest place of honor to the Lord.

As your child hears you pray, let him hear you thanking and praising God for what He has done, including the blessings of family and home, but then also let your child see you simply sit, stand, or kneel in silence as you bask in the presence of the Lord. Do not let your child interrupt you in these times of deep and holy reverie. Insist that he allow you to have this intimacy with the Most Holy One.

3. Guide your child in his selection of heroes. I am continually amazed at the number of children, teens, and even college students who have ungodly heroes. They keep photos of them in their rooms and they talk about them incessantly.

I once visited several of my students at an open house in their dormitory. I was very surprised to see a couple of posters on the wall depicting a movie star and a music group that had reputations as ungodly people.

I asked the young man, "Why did you choose these posters for your wall?"

He responded, "I like the work they do."

"Do you want to be like them?" I asked.

"Yeah, sure," he said. "Make millions, live in style, travel the world, have lots of gorgeous women around all the time. Who wouldn't want to be like them?"

"But do you *really* want to be like them?" I asked.

"What do you mean?" he said.

"Do you want to be the type of people they are?"

He responded defensively, "So what should I have on my wall . . . a picture of Jesus?"

"Not necessarily," I said. "But I would think you would want to look at something every evening and morning that inspired you to be who you really want to be."

A few months later, I went back to the dorms for another visit. This young man had different posters—one of the fluke of a diving whale and the other of a beautiful river in the high mountains. They were beautiful and inspiring images. I didn't say a word about them, but he did. "Don't get any ideas," he said with a grin, "I don't want to be a whale or a mountain."

"Oh, but I think maybe you do," I said. "Neither is a bad analogy of certain traits that are very noble in a man."

He only grinned.

When your child comes home telling you that he "loves" a certain rock group or movie star or that he wants to grow up to be just like a certain athlete . . . pay close attention. Probe his comments. What about that person does he like? Sometimes what he likes is the way the person combs his hair or the shape of the woman's body. At other times, it's a perception of fame, wealth, or power. Help your child distinguish between admiration and lustful desire. The former should be firmly rooted in evidence that the person is living a moral, God-fearing life. Lustful desire for an unknown person, especially a person of ill repute, should be strongly discouraged.

This is not judgment. It is discernment—discerning qualities of character and whether to emulate them or not. Judgment refers to passing a sentence on a person as worthy or unworthy, good or evil. Behavior is always to be subjected to discernment.

Always keep in mind that you are the one who has the

authority to govern what is displayed in your home. You have a right to determine what you will and will not allow to be kept in your child's room as long as you are financially or legally responsible for your child. Express to your child why you don't allow certain things and why you think your child needs to reevaluate his misappropriated affection.

Take it upon yourself to hold out a different set of role models to your child. Tell your child the stories of the saints of the past and their struggles and triumphs. Talk to your child about missionaries who have led godly lives as they took the gospel to remote regions of the world or current heroes who have stood against the tide for what they believed. Let your child know why you consider these to be people of good repute, true heroes of the faith.

Point out to your child that even people with sterling character have the capacity to disappoint us or make mistakes. Nobody is immune to temptation. We are to pray for those we admire that they might continue to be strong in their faith.

We can certainly pray for those who are living ungodly lives, but we must do so without any desire to follow in their footsteps.

4. Enjoy silence with your child. Not everything you do with your child needs to be analyzed. Some experiences are left best shrouded in mystery and silence.

One of the most deeply spiritual students I have ever had was Ruthie. She was a student of very few words, but what she said was always stated simply and profoundly. She gave a speech in one of my classes titled, "Grandma's Easter Bread." She told in detail what her grandmother had done each Easter in teaching her and her sister how to make the traditional family Easter bread, which was a glazed and fruited yeast bread. It was a recipe that Grandma had brought from Russia.

Ruthie concluded her speech, "None of us said a word the entire time Grandma measured, mixed, or showed us how to knead the bread. The bread was always made in silence. My sister and I always sensed a great sadness in my grandmother on that afternoon. After the bread went into the oven, she would read the story of Christ's crucifixion to us. And then we went outside to wait until the bread was out of the oven, cooled, and ready for glazing. As I recall it, we never felt much like playing. We usually just moped around until we could smell the bread coming out of the oven. It seemed to take forever for the bread to bake, even though it was only about an hour. Grandma never said a word about the bread until Easter morning, when she would hand us each a piece and say, 'The Lord is risen.' Our response, of course, was 'He is risen indeed.' And in our hearts, He truly was."

Ruthie's grandmother had allowed the very act of handling bread to become an act of worship. I could easily imagine her kneading and braiding those loaves as if she were handling the very body of Christ. An oven became a tomb. Resurrection became something tangible. And best of all, Grandma never needed to preach a sermon for her granddaughters to understand and fully absorb the meaning of Easter.

Share moments of silent awe with your child. Let the experience be the message.

5. Keep yourself and your children from idols. That is the final statement of John's letters: "Little children, keep yourselves from idols" (1 John 5:21).

An idol is anything we value more than our relationship with God. It is anything we set up as a substitute for God in our lives.

Idols are rarely inanimate objects, but they can be. A person may love that new car to the point that he spends all of his time thinking about it, polishing it, and driving it . . . to the point that he just can't imagine living his life without it. When the car becomes the most important determinant of self-concept, the car becomes an idol.

Idols are more often people—and specifically, people we dearly love. We tend to let our boyfriends and girlfriends, spouses, children, and dear friends take the place of God in our lives.

How so? We turn to them for advice and wouldn't dream of making a decision without their input. We arrange our schedules to fit theirs. We direct all devotion toward them. Our love turns into worship.

The greater danger is not that your child may make an idol out of a toy or a pet dog but that he make one of you, his parent.

Always point beyond yourself to God. Certainly you worked at a job to earn the money to put the bread on the table, but let your child know that it is God who gave you the ability to work. He provided the job for you, helped the farmer and baker make the bread, and guided you to get the best bread for your money!

You may feel that you are the one who has made your child who he is. In fact, it is God who has given you anything good that you have imparted to your child, and it is God who has been present in all good and healthy aspects of your relationship. Your child is His creation, initially and in an ongoing way.

Let your child know that you are trusting God to complete the good work that He has started in your child.

Let your child know that God alone is the One who never disappoints, who is always available, and who always seeks your child's highest good.

Let your child know that Jesus is the only perfect person who ever walked the face of the earth. He is your child's ultimate hero and role model.

Worship and Schooling

Send your child to school with the perspective that she is to respect her teacher and that, as she sees her teacher doing things that are truly godly, she should feel free to voice her admiration.

Do not in any way send a message to your child that he is to worship his teacher or that it is acceptable for him to desire a teacher in a sexual way. If you suspect your child is engaging in too much romantic fantasy about a teacher, take action immediately. Don't let your child be set up for a heartache or live in a fantasy world of false expectations.

Finally, don't let your child worship knowledge. Knowing about the world is no substitute for knowing the Creator and having a relationship with Him. Knowing how to do certain things is no substitute for knowing the One who can do everything.

Schools specialize in the "ees" of scientific studies: Psychology. Biology. Sociology. Botany. Chemistry. Physiology. Anatomy.

The "ee" subjects tend to give your child a feeling of power, so much so that many a young person arrives at a false conclusion: Studying what God *has done* is more worth my time than exploring who God is.

God is mystery. He cannot be fully comprehended. That flies in the very face of formal schooling. As your child studies his subjects, always point your child toward the greatest subject: God's love for your child. That love can't be put under a microscope or analyzed in a test tube. It can't be readily observed, charted, or measured. But it can be felt. And the truth of that subject is just as knowable as any scientific fact.

Teens often are fascinated by subjects such as comparative religions and philosophy. As your child studies about religions, always point her back to the source of all faith—God Himself. What your child knows objectively about world religions is never as valuable or potent as what she knows intuitively about the living Lord.

Furthermore, nothing the school system has to offer your child can result in his salvation. Schools prepare children for the here and now, not the hereafter. Schools prepare children to be their own salvation and to effect salvation for others. They do not prepare children to accept the saving grace of the Lord.

God is more powerful than any school system and wiser than any teacher. Continually point your child toward God as being the only acceptable object of his worship. He is the Lord, and no one else!

The Irony of Worship and Independent Thought

An amazing thing happens as a student becomes sure of his faith in God and truly worships Him. He tends to become much more independent as a thinker. He is far less likely to be blown about from philosophy to philosophy. The student with a strong faith in God has a stability of the intellect.

He knows what he believes because he knows in whom he believes. He knows what he thinks because he knows who created all there is to think about. He is patient in working his way through problems because he senses that the One who solves problems is on his side.

Those who do not know in whom they believe follow this guru or that. They wander from discipline to discipline and from idea to idea, always following the latest popular leader or fad.

Many parents believe that faith can make a child intellectually lazy, but a strong faith stimulates a child to become keen intellectually. The more a student has a sense of divine purpose stemming from a relationship with the Almighty, the more that student has a drive to succeed at the tasks he is pursuing.

Encourage your child to engage in worship. In so doing, you will be encouraging your child to learn as never before.

Chapter 16

CONCLUSION:

Life's Most Important Lessons Don't Happen in the Classroom

Three final statements remain to be said about your role as a teacher and your home as a place of learning.

1. The home is more than a classroom.

While your home is a classroom in the finest sense of the word, it is also a place where your child should feel abundantly safe and secure. The world is a big place full of new experiences. Home should be a place of familiarity. Don't continually press your child to learn. There's a time when your child needs to be allowed to "shut down" and rest. It is in rest that much of what your child has encountered is internalized.

Your home also needs to be a place of play—of hearty laughter and genuine rest and relaxation. Make your home a haven in which true re-creation—rejuvenation and restoration—is possible.

2. Teaching life's lessons happens over time and by a process described in Scripture as "here a little, there a little."

As a parent, you don't need to have a formal curriculum. Let life's lessons come up as life flows. Make them a seamless part of your expression to your child. In other words, there is no need to say, "Now, we are going to have a life lesson," or "This is an important lesson, so pay attention!"

Simply share principles and truths as you go about your

daily life, recalling experiences, making comments, and asking questions.

3. Your home and teaching should be based on objectives but without the pressure of examination.

Don't be quick to draw conclusions about your child's education. You may not have any sense that what you have taught has been received until your child is seventy years old and you are one hundred and one! The encouraging aspect of this lifelong classroom is that you have a privilege few teachers have—to see how your child turns out twenty-five years down the road.

It's Never Too Late to Start

If you feel that you are behind in teaching these lessons—perhaps your child is already a teen or young adult—you can still start teaching them today. You may even already be a grandparent. If so, take every opportunity available to teach these lessons directly to your grandchildren.

Should you have a sense that you have failed your teen or young adult by not teaching certain lessons in their childhood, apologize to your grown child. Let your child know where you think you may have made mistakes and how you hope to remedy them. Don't make promises that you can't keep, but do express your desire to encourage your child at this point in his or her life. Most likely your child will accept your apology with a heart willing to give you a second chance. He will value deeply your encouragement and love.

Lessons That Produce Good Students

In recalling our definition of a good student, let's see how it lines up with the lessons that are best taught by parents.

Good Student	Simple-Truth Lesson
Responsible	You are never alone, neither abandoned nor elevated above others.
Curious and creative Discerning Thoughtful (rational, with good language skills) problem-solving	You must always ask good questions if you want good answers and results.
Open-minded	You are what you take in.
Diligent	You grow through giving.
Optimistic	Rejoice!
Ambitious (in pursuit of excellence)	Keep learning.
Realistic but hopeful about the future	Behavior has consequences but forgive generously.
Decisive	You always have a choice.
Intellectually honest	Seek truth and speak truthfully.
Independent thinking	Choose carefully the object of your worship.

Good students don't just happen. They're taught, and, more important, they're trained. Training happens through repetition, including repeated application. Don't just teach a lesson once and hope it sticks. These life lessons should become second nature to your child. They should become a part of the way your child thinks and responds intuitively.

The reward of good teaching is a student's ability to pass

lessons on to the next generation. The reward of good parenting is the same. Your *child's* ability to teach life's most important lessons to your grandchildren will be your greatest reward. It's a reward worth pursuing with all your heart, mind, and spirit.